ELVIS
MONOLOGUES

ELVIS
MONOLOGUES

EDITED BY LAVONNE MUELLER

HEINEMANN
Portsmouth, NH

Heinemann
A division of Reed Elsevier Inc.
361 Hanover Street
Portsmouth, NH 03801-3912

Offices and agents throughout the world

Library of Congress Cataloging-in-Publication Data

Elvis monologues / edited by Lavonne Mueller.
    p. cm.
  ISBN 0-435-07044-4
  1. Presley, Elvis, 1935-1977--Drama. 2. American drama--20th century. 3. Monologues. I. Mueller, Lavonne.
  PS627.P74E45 1997
  812'.04508351--dc21   97-24665
                                     CIP

Editor: Lisa A. Barnett
Production: Melissa L. Inglis
Cover design: Tom Allen/Pear Graphic Design
Manufacturing: Louise Richardson

Printed in the United States of America on acid-free paper
01 00 99 98   DA   2 3 4 5 6 7 8 9

Contents

Introduction

Whose Elvis Is It, Anyway?

To read the monologues in this collection is to discover what Freud called the "dark continent" of icon psychology. These pieces unfold all the underpinnings of a complex national celebrity. Writing about Elvis myself, I find him a continual mystery. As I examine and reexamine these monologues, I am perpetually thrust into the etiolated landscape of the American Dream gone berserk.

Elvis is that symbol which is a papier-mâché structure built on the imagination and hopes of an American public nourished for decades on the peculiarly American Dream that every person is capable of becoming someone, that he/she can somehow become part of a world inhabited by beautiful people who were themselves once just one of the lowly, struggling masses. It is the fantastic lure and excitement of poor Elvis making it big that has lured so many to destruction on the commercial, cardboard rocks of Hollywood and the music world. The world of Elvis is fascinating to writers, I believe, because it is a world of illusion, drugged by yellow journalism, tabloids, and cinema. It's a personal world—a wasteland, in fact—where the illusionary hero must conform to the American code of success and deliver the goods to hungry spectators. It's the Horatio Alger myth, and the eternal middle-class ennui is sustained by gaudy spectacles. Nathanael West would ultimately place Elvis in the dream dump. According to West, the dreams of America finally come to rest in a *dream dump*—a graveyard of worn-out props and moving picture artifacts. The history of civilization comes to this—a mighty heap of hopes and aspirations thrown into a back lot like twisted auto bodies.

The "dream dump" has inspired many writers. Melissa Scott's mother got a wink from the King, and this is the "dramatic accident" that is the core of her monologue. Lanie Robertson has always been intrigued with what *isn't* Elvis—a kind of negative space—that is the germ for "I Ain't Elvis." Karen DeWitt remembers reading about the time Elvis got his first bike; that simple act transcends a normal childhood experience when it deals with an icon. Maureen McCoy is fascinated with Elvis and his relationship with food—"Baking for Life." As these writers and the others in this book attempt to learn about Elvis's identity, it's as if they are also becoming involved in the search for themselves. Elvis is the dramatic unexpected in their path. There is no doubting His influence—the King's persona and personalia is a tilting frenzied paradox that is somehow a vector to even one's own interior.

Reading these monologues, the mosaic of Elvis is still beautifully elusive. But brilliant facets are designed by each author who lets Elvis or a "witness" discourse freely and casually. When I was collecting this anthology, I did not want diatribes but rather chats from the ganglia. In these dramatic works are nerve endings, cavalier and testy, that transmit the daze, the brash, the gaudy, salty verve of every attempt against a real and unreal hero/antihero. As for myself, I believe when writing about the extraordinary, one must always emphasize the ordinary.

One is constantly aware of the presence of Elvis's music. It's as if it stands inside the book gleefully directing ideas and images like a policeman on a safe small island. It reminds me of Mallarmé and the poet's use of multiple meanings of words to paint a tablecloth that could also be a mountain. Such is the fusing of Elvis's songs.

I, too, have always been fascinated by Elvis. But my emphasis as a writer has constantly been on Elvis as a soldier. Who was this Star who went into the Army and wanted to be treated like a common grunt? How did He take orders from his sergeants and officers? Who was this King who ate in the mess halls with soldiers, slept next to them on a narrow cot in the barracks? What was He like pulling KP? Even though He later went into Special Services and was treated *special*, how did He get through intensive Basic Training?

I am convinced that risk is necessary for the writer to understand Elvis. The authors in this book enter in every change or angle of interpretation—as well as delivery. They feel they must keep the reader continually off-balance in front of their creation. Their Elvis is a wager kept riding on throws of the dice. Everything can be lost at any roll. When it can no longer be lost, the creation is finished. The writer is outside. Dangerous choices by the writers become as much a part of Elvis as his history. These dramatizations have ironically presented all the things that the real Elvis is and isn't.

Then, whose Elvis is it? Recently, a memorabilia dealer in London was sued by the Presley estate for the use of the King's name. Judge Hugh Laddie ruled that the Presley estate does not own "in any meaningful sense the words *Elvis* or *Elvis Presley*. Even if Elvis Presley was still alive, he would not be entitled to stop a fan from naming his son, his dog or goldfish, his car or his house *Elvis* or *Elvis Presley* simply by reason of the fact that it was the name given to him at birth by his parents," the judge wrote.

"Elvis is up there, somewhere, smiling down," said Sid Shaw when hearing the Judge's decision. Shaw sells Elvis trinkets in an east London shop called Elvisly Yours.

I guess we really always knew that Elvis belongs to us all. Now, it's even legal.

Lavonne Mueller

Saving Grace

CYNTHIA L. COOPER

Wearing a lab coat, Janeanne sits at a bare, unadorned desk, leaning across. Unseen is an investigator, to whom she speaks.

JANEANNE: I know what you want to know.

She suddenly leans back, closes her eyes for a moment, and begins to sway in her seat. She takes a deep breath, opens her eyes and begins to sing—demonstrating great feeling if minimal ability—the first lines of "Love Me Tender."

1956. Title of Elvis' first movie, too; same year. (*She hums*)

So you don't like my singing. I can tell by the way you look down at your pad, pretending there's some very important information you have to write down for the captain. Well, *you* don't like my singing, and *I* didn't like what they were doing to Elvis. So that's why I did something about it.

Oh, I heard when you said it's not about arrest. "You're merely conducting an investigation into potentially improper expenditure of government funds." What are you? FBI? Or was it the Food and Drug Administration—the FDA? Or did you say the FTC? Or the CDC? All those people in all those agencies with all those letters who are all interested in investigating DNA. And Elvis. And little old me.

Well, you can bust me if you want to. I don't care. All those letters get right to the heart of the problem. I saw it when I first went back into biology. I discovered that people had lost the feel of things.

Like take DNA. That's all wrong. Three lousy letters. It's

I

deoxyribonucleic acid. God, I love the sound of it so much. Deoxyribonucleic acid. Deoxyribonucleic acid. I feel like I'm making beautiful music every time I say it. And it's just one part. When you really get behind deoxyribonucleic acid—put your body and feeling and emotion under DNA—deoxyribonucleic acid—

—ahhh . . . that is fine. Really, really fine.

She says the last line as if She is in love.

But even really fine things need tender loving care.

She stands, as if stepping back into the lab.

The director gave a little seminar to all of us new people when I was first hired at the lab. (*She becomes the director*)

"One day because of our work on something invisible to the eye—DNA—we will begin to know the complete identity of humans. We will know every nucleotide, every A, C, G, and T inside the human body, all three billion elements of the interior code that define a person completely, making an exact blueprint for every human being."

Suffice to say, I was about the oldest one there. I'd come back to biology after having two kids. So maybe my understanding of history was a little different—at least on certain points. I'd sit and listen at lunch hour. (*She becomes three other technicians*)

"Imagine," said one, "if we could figure out the complete DNA code of one really famous person."

"Yeah," said another, "even if DNA has three billion elements, that's still quantifiable. It's not infinity."

"And there is money in it. People are willing to put up investment capital for DNA banks, that kind of thing."

"But you'd need one really famous person."

"There's Einstein . . ."

"Not splashy enough."

"Queen Elizabeth."

"No one really cares."

"Shakespeare."

"Too esoteric."

(*To investigator*) These names went round and round like a hound dog crying all the time, and, as I recall, that's when Elvis first came up.

(*As the characters*)

"Think about all the Elvis imitators."

"If—we could actually discover Elvis' complete DNA code—"

"And alter a person's genes to make a new Elvis, a real Elvis, someone with the exact genetic makeup of Elvis, we'd be—"

"Rich."

(*To investigator*) "Rich." That's what they said. How could they understand? Watson and Crick only discovered the double helix one year before "That's All Right, Mama." The people in the labs were so-o young. They had no perspective.

Think of it. If these people really understood DNA—or Elvis—they would listen to the words—roll them around in their mouths, let them melt under their tongues, and then let them out gently, mellifluously, with tenderness. Take the DNA bases. Even the director called them by their initials: A or G or C or T. When the words are so marvelous—"Adenine." "Guanine." "Cytosine." "Thymine." But all the people in the labs say are A or G or C or T. As if you could sing 'Don't be C' and that would suffice for "cruel" or 'don't step on my B Suede Shoes' and that would make up for "blue." No, I believe that people in the labs have no concept of the artistic.

Still, I didn't pay much mind. I took the lunch discussions as idle chatter. Because it didn't seem really possible. And then more and more things kept happening. New testing. New equipment. Funding. Grants. More genes on the genome were identified. The pace accelerated. And then one day people were huddled in a corner.

(Acting as other characters)

"If someone pretended to be a journalist and got an interview with Lisa-Marie, and then Lisa-Marie had something to drink, and we got the saliva off the rim of the glass, and extracted DNA . . ."

"You'd still only have offspring with Elvis and Priscilla's DNA. There's a better way. Elvis had a twin, but the twin died at birth. No one knows exactly where the twin is buried. But twins, if they are identical, have the *same* DNA. So if we went down to Tupelo with one of those laser probes, and found the body of . . ."

"Wait. We can keep it simple. If one of us visited Graceland and got a swab off an item of clothing—where he sweated, the armpits or collar, for example, on the gold lamé suit or the karate robe—we could test that."

(To investigator) I still didn't think anything of it. But then one day, one of the technicians mentioned that he was taking a vacation in Memphis. Everyone else nodded and smiled. I'm not paranoid. I saw it with my own eyes. My back stiffened. Elvis' song, "Don't," started pumping through my brain, as if he were singing to me personally.

(Confidentially) They were working on a secret plan to identify the entire genetic code of Elvis, which they planned to sell to a commercial entity for harvesting—to re-create Elvis. And it was happening right here in a research lab supported with government money.

(More voluble) I want you to understand one thing. I am not a fanatic. I am not one of those people who celebrates Elvis' birth and memorializes his death. I don't make pilgrimages to Graceland. But *they* didn't understand Elvis at all.

See, DNA, genes—they don't tell the whole story. Because you could know every vowel in "Love Me Tender" and sing every note, like I do. But you still wouldn't *be* Elvis. You still wouldn't have that wonderful curl at the end of a phrase, that little hiccup of delight that injects surprise, that deep boom and slow slide up, the saving grace, that made Elvis. Notes don't make a song, and you could name all the genes in a person's body, but you wouldn't have a singer. You wouldn't have his smile; the eyes that could take in an audience; his soul.

After this technician came back, my suspicions grew. I noticed a group of people working late each night. There were hushed conversations, passed notes, winking and blinking. They always seemed intent on ushering me out the door as soon as possible at the end of the workday.

I watched this for several days. And then I couldn't take it anymore. While they were at lunch, I snuck to the back and stole the key to the locked refrigerator from one of the drawers. Then I opened the refrigerator. And just as I suspected there were fresh vials in there. Vials marked "E," like "E-1," "E-2," E-3." You know what that meant.

And there were notes on one of the tables. Had "G Information" on them, and that stood for Graceland. My suspicions were confirmed.

After that, I didn't waste any time. I knew what I had to do. I had to save Elvis.

I took the "E" "1-2-3" vials, stuck them in my shirt, checked out with the guard, flashing my badge, of course, and walked out the door, down to the strip—the commercial strip—looking for the right place. I came to a toy store and I knew that's what he wanted. I could hear him singing to me, "I only want to be your teddy bear." I poured out the vials on the sidewalk. 1-2-3. And then I smashed the vials. 1-2-3. I destroyed private property. And then I tore up the notes into little bits, and destroyed some more.

And I'm the one who left all those no-name messages with you and every other highfalutin agency I could think of and said there was something you ought to know. You're just the first to show.

But I don't care if you know my name anymore. "I don't care if the sun don't shine." Because there will be only one King. (*Hums "Love Me Tender." Sits back down*)

The name's Janeanne.

So does that answer all of your questions?

At RaeDean's Funeral

MELISSA SCOTT

It's 1977 or '78. Willie is young, late teens/early twenties, with long hair like a heavy metal guitarist that he's tried in vain to subdue to match his Sears suit and the solemn occasion.

WILLIE: I want to thank y'all for letting me speak here today. For those of you that don't know me, I'm RaeDean's boy Willie—from before she married Sam? So, like I said, I appreciate you letting me speak here—I figure you didn't have to do it, 'n I'm grateful, 'cause I know Mama would've wanted me to be here if I could. I been listening to everything everybody said, and it's been real nice. You said stuff about Mama—like her being in the choir and all that?—that I didn't know.

But I guess I want to talk about the stuff everybody knows about—like me—'n maybe it's not proper here in the church, but y'all know it anyway, so I figure I might as well tell it right.

Elvis winked at my mama—yeah, I know, y'all heard *that* story fiftymillion times, but it was her favorite, and somebody's got to tell it at her funeral.

How it happened was, she and Carolynn Pierce wanted to go to Memphis to look for a dress for the Summer Ball. Carolynn's cousin Jamie was going anyway, and he said he'd drive them, so he dropped them off at Goldsmiths and said he'd be back in a couple hours. But they got done a lot faster than that and they decided that they would go out to Graceland, because Elvis was in town. So when they walked up to the gate, there were people there like there always were, and they just kinda stood there, looking at the house and wondering what it'd be like inside. How Elvis would've made it nice for his mama, and what it was like now that he was home again and it was his. And I guess there was more people there than usual, 'cause all of a sudden there he was, walking down the drive and over the lawn to see what was going on. Mama said there was four or five guys with him, little guys, not big and mean, guys that you see with him in all the photos, and he and them just walked down to the gate like they were—well, like they were ordinary. He was dressed nice, she said, not like kids, singers, now, and he was smiling, like he was glad to see them all, but a little embarrassed, too, like somebody who couldn't remember if he'd invited you by after all.

So of course everybody sort of surged forward, and shrieked and called, and he came down all the way to the fence and started shaking hands with people. And Carolynn got up to the front somehow, with the book with the fabric samples, and she stuck that through the fence screaming, "Elvis, Elvis, please sign my book."

Mama didn't have anything for him to sign, but she pressed up close to Carolynn anyway, and she was glad she did because he did come over. He took the book—which was one of those little cardboard things, with three or four pieces of fabric stapled in it, so Miz Pierce could look it over and decide what was appropriate? And he looked at it kind of funny and said, "'scuse me, but, uh, this is dress goods."

Carolynn gave him her best smile and said, "Uh-huh, and I'll sew it in my dress for the Summer Ball—whichever color you like best."

Mama said he smiled back, and took the ink pen and the book and scrawled his name across the top piece—which was the one Carolynn liked best anyway, which is a good thing. But then, as he was handing it back and about to move on to the next person, he looked past Carolynn and he saw Mama. Their eyes met, and she said she didn't know what to do. I mean, that was Elvis, Elvis Presley, standing not a yard away from her, just as good-looking, and sexy, as she'd ever imagined, and sweet, too, to be there at all. But she managed a smile, and his smile widened, got just a little hint of the devil in it, and he winked at her.

And then he went on.

Y'all know the rest of it. Mama and Carolynn came on back home, and Carolynn sewed that sample swatch into her ball dress—and into her wedding dress, too—and Mama got asked to the Summer Ball after all and I was born that spring.

But what I want to say is, I've heard a lot of talk all my life, how Mama wasn't all that pretty—how she was just plain ugly, and never learned how to handle herself, so she said yes to the first boy who asked her to dance and then for more. And that's why she had me before she was married, and why all she ever got for a husband was big ol' Sam Ball who just didn't care as long as the dinner got cooked and washed up after.

But lookahere. *Elvis* winked at my mama. *Elvis* thought my mama was pretty enough to smile at her and give her the wink of his eye. She was pretty to him that day up in Memphis, and that ought to be pretty enough for Sam or anybody in this whole town.

Baking for Life

MAUREEN MCCOY

Stout woman in her eighties wearing full-length apron. In kitchen, mixing bowl on small table. She is mixing in a rhythmic fury, humming "Bossa Nova." She pauses, shakes her old body, moving around the table, finally lifts a spoon full of batter and squawks into it like a mike. Sighs. Takes a nice long lick off the spoon. Remembers she is not alone.

It beats the heck out of me why anyone would come begging an old woman to make a show of mixing up cakes. Most people just wants to eat them. But I hear things too. I hear you latest Elvis diggers got to go beyond the crowds over at Graceland, make yourself some discovery around here. You sniff out the pound cake lady—like I can set you right. I'll say it once: butter, sugar, flour, whipping cream, and more eggs than a body eats in a week. That's the Elvis pound cake. Cold oven, let it rise gradual to the high heat. Don't add nothing afterward unless you've got homemade vanilla ice cream on hand.

Five hundred strokes. I got me a ways to go here.

Them two New Yorkers is the ones first found me out, but I can say that they kept me out of the lights, part of the deal. No name, please, or every last Tupelonian's gonna have me baking up their birthday cakes. This here's the only cake I make and, unless I hit a real blue streak, the only time's at his birthday and Christmas. It'd been that way about all his life, and after Gladys died you can bet it meant the world to Elvis for me to keep on. I don't know nothing about bananas and whatever else they got to stuffing him with. I only baked the cakes, his baby boy cakes. Later, I'd come over from home, to

Memphis, delivering him the cakes. Sometimes I seen him and sometimes I didn't, but he always called up afterward and said, "Thank you, ma'am" in a boy-voice. Food can take you back. Put a candied yam in front of me and I'm a squealing baby girl in mama's arms all over again. Everyone wants their mama, no matter what their age. And I give Elvis that, the touch of his mama and the sweet baby days. That's what I give him, all through the years. Times when he was in trouble I'd have half a mind to send over more cakes—soothe the boy—but I never did want to intrude none either. Still, it's a long time from his January birthday on back to Christmas. I'd have about a whole year on my hands before I could give him more cakes.

Vanilla extract. I forgot to say it. Eggs room temperature. This here recipe goes back to my grandmother and there wasn't no Frigidaire humming and sucking up electric in her day.

The New Yorkers found me out when I come over to Graceland delivering cakes to his people. Since his passing, I've taken the cakes over there faithful these twenty years anyway, every birthday and Christmas, and the anniversary of his passing, too. I wouldn't think of skipping. And there they sat, like waiting for bomb alert, New Yorkers down here, the girl as starved-white as a body can be, looking to find people eating potato chip sandwiches, bologna fried in bacon grease, and whatnot, for their recipe book. They's eyes looked like y'alls, shiny with luck, and they's being demure, which even I knew was an act and a half. They's saying "ma'am this" and "ma'am that," taking cues from the gent I deliver the cakes to who says it in a natural Memphis voice.

Into the oven, lovelies. Cold oven. Two cakes at once.

Now the bowl may be licked. Here's your spoon, but first I'm a tell you one thing to take back and chew on. Elvis' last birthday I swooped the cakes into the oven and turned around to lick the bowl myself, and what do I find in the bottom of this here CorningWare 1953 large-size mixing bowl? The yellow one that nests green and red and baby blue inside it? I seen the face of Elvis in the batter, that's what. The scrapings in the bottom was all glistening gold. I seen the future. I knew it was the time, the year in which Elvis would be passing from earth.

Weren't nothing I *could* do! Alert someone? Tell Elvis? I was an auntie-mama, a cake baker from home, mind you. I'd known him since he was two years old, but I weren't nobody to go straight up to Elvis *the King* and scold him. That batter-face in my bowl was smooth, chilly smooth like something Egyptian, far gone, marble eyes, a sign of the Lord's calling, this goldfaced Elvis. Knowledge was fierce upon me.

(*Taps bowl sharply with spoon*) This here's the bowl. I didn't lick it that time. I didn't scrape none, either. I took one long look and then ran warm water and let all the signs rise and fade in bubbles and streams. Ain't no reason to look on the dead, as far as I'm concerned. You live with folks, or you pray to them in heaven, no sense in looking and looking on anyone dead.

Go on and lick! Ain't no face in that batter. No signs gonna jump at you and change *your* life.

Smell them cakes—sweet as fruit. Of course you could faint, honey. They's toned it down so much in your bakeries, they's added so much air and waste and contrivance to your cakes, even the smell is near down to zero. This here's *cake!* Sliding right out of the pans, not a crumb lost. You look at that.

Cooling just a titch now. There. Don't need no frosting. You got your cake and I got mine. I give you that cake to eat. Eat it like a prayer, honey, hands working round it this a-way, cupped. First slice you got to feel burning in your hands. Put your face down to it. Burning hot, yessir. Hot like a heart, steam rising.

(*Takes a bite, closes eyes*) My sweet Jesus. (*Turns away*) Sorry, this here's private business. I have my mumbo jumbo, things I think while eating the cake of Elvis. (*Speaks between bites and often with mouth full*) I'm a old woman. (*Beat*) This cake goes back least as far as my granny. (*Beat*) You can figure the numbers. (*Beat*) This cake's seen war and peace. (*Beat*) We's long livers, the family of this cake. In the beginning I just passed the sweetness on to the little boy Elvis, neighborly I did. I expect there later I was praying to Jesus that the cakes he loved so well might be The Way, and that by eating my whipping cream pound cake Elvis'd hitch onto the star of us old long livers, the bunch. Then I seen the batter-face.

Lord, this cake takes me back, way back. I'm a small girl, eating this cake. I always eat one cake before I take the others to Graceland. But during Elvis' time, I used to give him his cakes first, and then come back home to eat mine same time I figured Elvis was eating his. Elvis had a funny way of eating his cake. He'd stack one piece on top of another, turn them sideways and hold on tight. He ate across, the way you do with sweet corn. Something he started on little, looking cute, holding his yellow cake same as a ear of corn. I think hard on Elvis-above while I eat. I hope to my Jesus he is reliving the sweet sweet days of being a boy. Always such a sweet sweet boy. (*Turns back to visitor*)

Hey! No you don't, honey. You don't stop eating Elvis cake after a prissy bite or two. What kind of shame you pulling on me? You tuck into it, yessir. You gonna eat the whole thing before you get up off that chair. That's right, you gonna work while you're here. What do you think *I'm* doing, ninny? I'm a fork it into you now. There, and there and there, you want to know something of Elvis. We're going faster now, faster down the hatch, Little Yankee Priss. More cake, the whole thing. You hurt, eating this cake. You choke. Nodding your head that's right, you hurt. You eating it all, honey. Faster than you can think. You got nothing to say, eating Elvis cake. Feel what it's like. You got nothing.

Heart of a Dog

TERRY GALLOWAY

When I was a kid living in Berlin, do you know what we believed in? Not Art. Not God. Elvis Presley. He was just another sweet GI stationed in cold-war Germany but we thought, "Saved! The Russians, they ain't gonna bomb us. Not with Elvis Presley here! This guy's the King!" Ah, Jesus, when I think of where we were—Berlin, where holocaust was not inconceivable. When we left that city, it was no vacation trip, we had to get out. We left by train in the dead of winter in the dead of night. And when we approached the Russian border the train slowed and I woke up. I poked my head out into the corridor and I saw, yes, the Russian guards with their machine guns slung over their shoulders. But they were wearing these fur hats that looked like animals. And there was a string of lights marking the border, like tiny, white Christmas lights. And the snow was six feet high, glittering under that string of lights, glittering. The guards could have marched my Daddy off the train. They could have taken us, too. They could have shot us all and ignited the cold war. I knew all this. But the lights, the snow . . . it was so merry, so Christmasy I just couldn't be afraid.

And my mother says she wasn't afraid then, either. It wasn't until we got back to the States and suddenly all you heard was Berlin! The Wall! Berlin! The Bomb! Berlin, Berlin, Berlin as if it rhymed with The End The End The End. And that's when she was afraid. Not so much by where we were at the moment, but where we so unknowingly had been.

Did we really think Elvis could save us from all that? From anything?

It scares me to think of it . . . the things we hold on to.

Just Look to Your Right

GAY DAVIDSON-ZIELSKE

That's right, ma'am. I'm the one you've been edging out with your elbow for the greater part of an hour now. I'm that smoky smell that crinkles your sculptured little nose there. Your mother's greatest heartbreak—the rebel who's never been any good. Take a peek—I have a slight undercut to my jaw, actually, like a pike. I have those jelly lips and that pancake makeup skin. My five o'clock shadow is like chocolate sprinkles on a too-sweet cupcake. Now, hold it, sugar. Don't you look down.

I'm telling the bartender in a voice too loud what it is I do. It's happy hour, so he only half hears what it is—so I repeat, "I impersonate the King." As usual, he looks me up and down, registers the lamb chop sideburns and says, "Pre–Service King, huh?" I allow as how it's the "Young Elvis" stamp image I'm interested in being. "So what does the King want to drink?" he asks. He himself doesn't look like anybody. In fact, he looks like everybody in this Europo-Scandinavian town. Healthy, milk-fed, pinkish blond. I resent his tone, so I manufacture a curled sneer. (I wonder if the King just had something caught in his tooth? Like a popcorn shell, for instance. He sneered, the cameras popped, it caught on. Of course, people who think like that—who want to tear him down like the Berlin Wall—probably also think his famous twisty hips came from a rectal itch. I have more respect than that.)

Now, you're looking at me in a confused way. I hold my glass up. "Elvis," I mouth. Now you're a pretty little thing and you actually blush. Sandra Dee blushed and that was the last girl I remember blushing.

15

"Elvis," I say out loud. "Down at the end of Lonely Street—Heartbreak Hotel. Down in the Ghet-t-t-o. Love me tender, but don't step on my blue suede shoes. You ain't nothin' but. . . ."

I can't tell a pretty girl to her face she's a dog. "Cryin' in the Chapel," I say. "Blue Moon of Kentucky."

"Elvis who?" you ask. "Costello?"

I'm the slight paunchy guy walking home with the guitar slung across his leather tasseled back.

Firehouse Rock

SHELLEY BERC

We see the shadow of Elvis with his guitar in profile in the dark-
ness. He lights a cigarette and is illuminated in shadow by the
lighter's flame. We hear him sing/speak in voice-over.

I see only when the town's afire.
I see only by the flashlight fire
by red light district fire
only
by stop lights
and ambulance lights
and ruby red candlelight.
I see red. My life sees red
red for danger.

Lights full up on Elvis. He is dressed as a fireman and is playing
his hose like a guitar and singing.

I been a grown man since four
and a kid forever more.
I got a thousand gals a-yowling
and ten thousand guys a-scowling.
Well, I'm a fireman, Mama
Drivin' you up that ol' fire wall.
A fireman, mister sister
A fireman, that's all.

I got my big red armored truck
and my hard red hat for luck.
Got my quick silver hose

and a siren that won't let go.
Well, I'm a FIREMAN, baby
born to drive you so loco.
I'm a fire-man, darling
A fireman, that is all.

I'm your red hot lickin' chicken
I'm your pure white jet stream jet
I'm your strike anywhere match man
and you're the blaze I mean to set.
Well, I'm a fireman, ladies!
Don't go and try to steal my flame. NO!
Well, I'm the Burn King, butter. LORD!
You ain't never gonna be the same.

Well, all you sugar babies
I'm coming straight to your rescue.
When the kindling in your fireplace gets so low
it stifles you.
Well, I'm your red hot savior
aimed to melt down your good behavior.
Yeah I'm your F-I-R-E WORKS Man
A fireman, that is all.

Canned applause. Elvis bows, graciously says, "Thank you, thank you all for coming tonight." He takes off his satin fire hat and his sequined fire coat, lays down his rock and roll hose, strips off his oxygen tank, takes a very rare cheeseburger out of his pocket and begins to eat.

I always been attracted to fire. Ever since I was a little kid and my daddy took me out into the woods. Well Daddy—he lit up his pipe and said: "Boy," he said, "Boy, it's hard to be a man. In fact. Point of fact. It is not easy to be a man. Walk with your head held high and your feet planted wide. Know when to find and know when to run, when your fun gets you on the wrong side of a gun. And in that case, in that case, leave a burning blaze, smoke filled haze behind you, right behind you."

Well, while he was stoking up the hype,
a meteor landed in his pipe.
Daddy's body blew up like a cat belly pup
turned to fire, all afire
little chariots of fire raging round his head
like a boogie-woogie baby in a rock'n'roll bed.
He sank in the flames
I leapt to my feet
jumping to the beat of that sweet funeral pyre
juice of the liar
higher and higher.

But Mama got to be a real drag. I love my mama. I really love Mama. But after Daddy died, she turned in her will to survive. She cried day in, cried day out. Poor old leaky bucket blew her water saver spout. And you know, you can't fight water with water so . . . one night, pitch black as a panther in tights, I crept out of bed, squeezed into my best asbestos and lead and torched that old home onto the range.

I took off above the tree line, over the rainbow. Christ, I was pretty up there. I found this cave where it's warm and still . . . big enough to dig my own grave in. When in the distance what do I see but the weirdest looking dude, all curled up, chained to a bounder like a rabid beast mumbling something about buzzards chomping out his liver. Well, I liked his heat and those blue Waikiki Beach movie eyes enough to decide not to die for a while. Besides, him and me, we shared this special love: ripping off the gods above. So he took me under his left wing and I joined the Brotherhood of Burning. We don't eat a blessed thing, supposed to live off air and alchemy. And sex . . . here? There ain't no such thing. We've hit the highest knowing man ever can: How to wrestle fire without burning our hands.

(*He sings*)

I stole fire from the mountain top
I stole fire from the volcano's mouth
I stole fire from the coral sea.
I stole fire and it set me free
Fire to fire to eternity.

Holy Knights of the Grill, that's us. Battling renegade microwaves, melting down the nuclear freeze. A sacred society, trained to ride the wings of lust but never never never give up our chastity . . . to feel the heat's supposed to be enough. But this ex on sex is messing up my spiritual progress. I mean . . . I got certain powerful associations between females and heat. I can't set a thing on fire. I'm consumed with desire. In short—burned up! When suddenly . . . there she is! Sweet sixteen. Virgin Queen. I invite her to a barbecue lunch and there and then I set her up.

(*He sings*)

Oh see her transcendence
In her orange glow
Come on, let's go.
Fire.

I wanted to engrave you a love song baby not burn you up like loco crazy. Just wanted to see you for a while all golden and lit up like an Olympic Torch, racing to the sky in flight of pain. Hey! When I saw your comet tail I just couldn't pray for rain. You burned too fast, too fast and free. And now, now you're gone, some Cinder-ella in the stars, falling on the sea, stroking over water, touching memory in me. I didn't mean to set you so high. Didn't mean to turn my back so long awhile. My timing's always left something to be desired. And mistakes, mistakes like this are tragic—The difference between love, love and magic. Fine line long haired sugar. Fine line crack line erupture sugar. Lady of dust and deep desire thou art forever after mine. My funny little holograph valentine. You Halley's Comet. You last cha cha in moonlight. You lady lost in waiting. Waiting for death and me. Waiting for us to set you free. Oh, love, you asked for it, begged and danced for it. I gave you my heart, gave you my studded soul. You're flying all right, lost in uranium glow.

Elvis and My Little Brother

JAN BUTTRAM

Place: a small town diner, East Texas. Time: now. Tiny Pickins, 58, speaks to her teenage son.

TINY: You want a coke? Hamburger? You got a full tank of gas? Did you check the oil? You going dressed like that? Is Loretta Sims going with you? Lord God. Well, sit down here a second. (*Beat*) Did I ever tell you that Elvis Presley sang for my little brother? He did. No, it wasn't a command performance. My brother introduced his act, you impudent little know-it-all! Because my little brother was president of his senior class. That's why. It happened at the high school gymnasium, not two miles from here in 19 and 52. Elvis wasn't a big star yet. He was just some little shrimp with a bunch of hair. And he was touring these little old high-school gyms, playing his guitar and singing sort of sexy church songs. He didn't have no Jordinnaires nor backup band nor glitter jeans or diamond belts. He wore blue jeans and picked an old guitar. Real simple. Rock 'n' roll hadn't even been invented—leastwise not for white folks. Elvis was inventing an American art form right then, right in front of all these kids. (*Beat*) Good God, no. There weren't no black people in the audience. This was before integration. We're talking 1952. Didn't you study history? They don't teach history anymore. That's why everyone is so messed up. I mean, you're a smart kid. You should study this shit. (*Beat*) I didn't have to study it because I was there, I can remember it. But that's not the point. The point I'm trying to make here is some things don't change. That's what I'm trying to tell you, just have some patience.

See, Elvis was to be onstage at 10:00 in the morning and

he was starving 'cause he didn't get into town soon enough to find anything to eat and my little brother, he give Elvis half of his peanut butter and banana sandwich and Elvis said, "Boy, you got good taste." Because Elvis liked peanut butter and banana sandwiches a lot. Everybody knows this. This is a recorded fact.

So, now then, when Elvis walked on the stage, my little brother introduced Elvis and shook his hand in front of the whole school . . . and, back then, even before he got famous, everyone thought Elvis was great. The girls loved Elvis. And because they loved Elvis, they all wanted to get close to my brother because he shook hands with him and give him half his sandwich. So, later, after Elvis got to be a big star, my brother felt special. Why? And dang it, I told you. Because the girls—and, hell, everybody, made a big to-do over it . . . he and Elvis were like equal for a split second.

My little brother told me later on, he knew, I mean he *knew*, that Elvis was good but he didn't know he was going to be a star or he woulda got his autograph. When did you get so sullen? I'm going to stop talking to you. (*Calling out*) Lavonne, warm up my coffee when you get a chance. Thank you, ma'am.

It comes to me, this afternoon sitting here waiting because you're late meeting me, I'm sitting here staring out at the city limits sign and thinking about this, and you, because you remind me of my little brother, you do . . . you're a lot like him, and it comes to me—the reason my little brother got the big head was because he met Elvis, and right after that, Elvis got to be a big star. And my brother figured something like that was going to happen to him—and then he up and left town, decided he had to go to college and all. Now, you got to be really careful thinking you're something special, because life comes looking for you. And just because you get to speak to somebody who gets to be big time, it don't mean that your life is going to be big time. It could mean that it ain't going to be nothing. Because they might be room for everyone at the top but you can't prove it by me. You can't prove it by my little brother either. He never got anywhere close to the top. A semi smashed him flat on Highway 82. And I never got there. I never got farther than that city limit sign because losing my brother scared that want-to right outta me.

Now, you're a young piece of shit, and you think nothing bad is ever is going to happen to you. You think you're damn invincible. Well, you best watch out. Because even if you was to get somewhere, you never know how long you'll be there. Elvis got somewhere—for a long time he got somewhere but the way they tell it, being at the top never made a goddamn. All he really enjoyed was the singing.

Of course, I worship him. I'll worship him my whole life. Not because he was the King of Rock 'n' Roll, but because he shook hands with my little brother. That made him worth a goddamn. So, go on . . . spend every last dime you have in your pocket to hear Pearl Jam or whoever it is. You're 16— you make your own money. Who am I? I'm just your god-damn mother. What the hell do I know. All I know is, I finally give up trying to eat peanut butter. Makes me misty-eyed when I bite into it. Damn near every time.

I Ain't Elvis

LANIE ROBERTSON

A Man stands alone on stage. He is singing the end of a song as the lights come up on him. He is accompanying himself on a guitar. He looks exactly like the old Elvis. He wears his hair in a coal-black, slicked-up pompadour. He wears very dark sunglasses, which he never removes. He wears cowboy boots and a white jumpsuit elaborately decorated with sequins. His fingers are covered in what appear to be diamond or rhinestone rings. Around his neck are heavy gold chains and several long scarves. He sings the chorus to "Hound Dog." He ends the number, stops singing, and bows, and wipes his brow and face with one of the scarves about his neck, then tosses it to the audience.

MAN: Thank ya. Thank ya. Thank ya so much. I sure do appreciate it. That was "Hound Dog." That lil number's one of my big hits. It's called "Hound Dog."

An' basic'ly it's about this mountain man who's a hunter, talkin' to his no-good huntin' dog. You can know that 'cause of the last line of the lyric: YOU AIN'T NEVER CAUGHT A RABBIT AN' YOU AIN'T NO FRIEND OF MINE.

He takes a snort from a pint bottle.

Now, maybe all you little girls an' boys know but basic'ly, a hunter's bes' friend's his dog. In this case a hound dog, which is, as you may know, not one of your pedigreed dogs but more of your Heinz 57 Varieties kinda dog. That's a dog born out in the sticks somewhere's under a porch or shed somewhere's out back prob'ly where the bitch has gone, that's the mother dog, see, bitch ain't a derogatory term for a dog, or

. . . I should say . . . isn't, but bitch is what you call your basic female dog when she has a passle ah puppies. You know, a litter? That is a bunch of puppies. Okay, what she does is, she us'ly goes off somewheres an' hides so the farmer or rancher or whatever, don't find her litter of puppies an' drown 'em all in the crick, which is how those folks pronounces what you an' me'd call us a creek or little river. So, this hunter, an' he's probably no serious hunter, just a "goin' out to shoot a few squirrels" kinda hunter so what he's sayin' is this dog, his dog, is a particularly sorry dog because he ain't never caught a squirrel. Or. In this case a rabbit. So what I'm doin' in this song is, I'm reprimandin', that is, I'm talkin' down to the dog. Not too harsh, though. I don't want any of you kids to get the idea that I'm mistreatin' my dog, 'cause I ain't. I mean, cause I'm NOT. See. What I'm doin' in the song is . . . I'm TRYIN' to get on my dog's tail. . . . Let me rephrase that, what I'm doin' is . . . tryin' to ENCOURAGE a better attitude outta my dog, see, so basic'ly he'll do a better job huntin'.

Now, the Birthday Boy here . . . Birthday Boy! Say . . . Birthday Boy! Can some one of you kids in the back . . . would you just . . . punch or tap or knock the hell outta the Birthday Boy on the . . . Hey! HEY! ARE YOU LISTENIN' TO ME OR WHAT? That's better. Now . . . Birthday Boy! I chose to sing that song especially for you cause you got that new puppy there for your birthday. No. No, no, now I wouldn't put the puppy in with the goldfish if I was you. He don't wanna drink from the goldfish. Oh, well's none of my business. But you best not put him in with the . . . THERE YOU GO! Oh, well. Somebody better pick up those goldfish. Well, if he's eatin' 'em, okay. Fish never hurt dogs. Anyhow . . . another reason I sing this song 'cause it express how I feel about a lot of different topics. For one, I sing it 'cause I DO sing it very good. And another is I think the song's symbolic of a lotta shit that goes down between women an' men nowadays. Least that's so of a lotta women been trapsin' their fat

26

asses in an' outta my bed lately.

But the main thing here I wanna tell you, girls an' boys, 'fore your parents come back in the room, is I wanna level with you here.Now listen up: I AIN'T ELVIS.

Now I know little, what's your name? Richard? Dick? Little Dickie? I KNOW Elvis is your Mom an' Dad's personal favorite an' they wanted special for me to come here to your fifth birthday party this afternoon with all your little friends here to sing for you because your Mom an' Dad think I look an' sound like Elvis. As a matter of fact your Momma tol' me if she didn't know Elvis was dead . . . but I ain't suppose to tell you that . . . she'dda SWORE I WAS HIM. But the truth of the matter is I AIN'T ELVIS an' I don't give a poot in a whirlwind who knows it. Basic'ly, and if the truth were known, I'm pretty pissed off with these people like your uptight asshole of a Mom an' Dad for just ASSUMIN' that I AM a Elvis imposter-look-alike-imitator. That is pure bull-crap an' I don't care who knows it. Now, I wouldn't tell that to your Mom an' Dad if I was you, 'cause they went to all this trouble an' expense ah fixin' up this whole deal here of a party for you an' all your nice little friends here . . . HEY! Get your cotton-pickin' little fingers offah that guitar-case, little girl, 'fore I come over there an' break your little neck. Then you'll REALLY look funny! Be in one of them neck-braces for the rest of your nat'ral life!

Yeah, I mean you, sweetie! Now shut up an' sit down an' keep your hands to yourself 'fore I come over there an' smack ya. Don't yer mama teach you to keep yer cotton-pickin' hands off other people's property or what? Shit! What's motherhood comin' to's what I wanna know.

Any-who, as I was sayin', I AIN'T ELVIS. I ain't even a ELVIS LOOK-ALIKE in my book. I mean, I didn't say that to your folks, Little Dickie, an' I'd appreciate it if none of you little kiddies'd do that either, 'cause, as I say they wanted to give you a nice party an' all. An' also they're payin' me a nice piece of change 'cause they said one of little Dickie's heroes is the dead Elvis, an' I figure he is for them too judge-ipatin' on your daddy's slicked-up hair and as one can see by all these homemade kinda paintings of Elvis all around this rumpus room in ever kinda garb he ever had on save a hard-on that mustah been painted by . . . who? Who did these pitchers, Dickie? Your Mom? Mom AND Dad! Well, your Dad's hair alone could stand the test, cain't it. Now what I want all of you to know is I AIN'T ELVIS. And furthermore I ain't never CLAIM to be ELVIS or even a ELVIS LOOK-ALIKE. See, when your Mom an' Dad come up to me in the Mall an' ask if they can hire me to perform some of my hits for a bunch of you shitty-assed little birthday party goers, well, hell, piss, shit, an' hail Mary! Who'm I to turn down a paycheck? I said, Hell yes! Here's one I don't even have to report to Uncle Sam while I'm at the same time drawin' my unemployment from Uncle Sam due to bein' laid off from the Graceland Bar an' Grill for tellin' the bossman to heat his suggestion that I add more Elvis' numbers to my Elvis Act to a cherry-red an' shove it up his ass! I mean, I AIN'T ELVIS an' I AIN'T GOT NO ELVIS ACT.

Now . . . now . . . now don't get me wrong. I KNOW I LOOK a little LIKE Elvis. But I was born with that look. I mean, do you think I stood in front of the mirror all through my high school years TRAININ' my lips to curl up like this? Hell no! I mean, shit no! I mean, DAMN! My mouth just NAT'RALLY DOES THAT. An' yes, I like to wear these shades, that is sunglasses, which you can see because my eyes is sensitive to light. 'Specially if I'm drinkin', which I don't mind if I do . . .

He takes a snort from a pint bottle.

But only on account of Little Dickie, the Birthday Boy's daddy was gentleman and kind enough to slip me this little pint bottle so's I could face up to performin' TWICED in one afternoon. I mean, FIRST of ALL for all ah you PLUS your Mommies and Daddies, beforehand, and now AFTER for all you little snot-noses while your Moms an' Dad's are UPSTAIRS playin' strip poker or playin' SWAP meat in the spare room for all I know. I mean, they SAID it's Canasta, but who knows? They didn't invite ME to their party. So HELL, I feel I owe it to all ah you, a whole new generation of ELVIS FANATICS to set you straight on the one thing: I AIN'T ELVIS.

He takes a snort from a pint bottle.

Yeah, it's true I DO sing songs most or all ah which the so-called KING recorded, but the reason I do is THOSE SONGS IS THE SONGS THAT EXPRESS WHO I AM.

Just like stickin' the head of that brand-new Birthday puppy in the goldfish bowl express who Little Dicky, the Birthday Boy, really is! So too it is with singin' "Don't You Step on my Blue Suede Shoes" or . . . "Heartbreak Hotel" or . . . "When My Blue Moon Turns to Gold Again" express who I am. An' who I am is . . . I AIN'T ELVIS!

An' hey! Why do I DRESS LIKE ELVIS? Answer is . . . I DON'T. I dress like ME. I tried all KINDS ah looks an' clothes an' what-not an' I discover I LOOK MY BEST LOOKIN' LIKE THIS! So . . . HEY!

He takes a snort from a pint bottle.

For one thing, I ain't FAT enough to dress like Elvis.

Another goll-durn thing . . . I don't even LIKE Elvis.

He wasn't no King in my book.

An' what's the goll-durn big deal about him shootin' out his TV whenever he seen somethin' he don't like on it? I myself have kicked the shit outta TWO TV sets. The las' one in my own Daddy's trailer-house. An' I would agin, 'cept the last time I did the glass tube broke an' cut right through my best pair ah genuine snakeskin leather shit-kickers, an' slice open the shit outta my right foot, an' my own Daddy threwed me outta his friggin' trailerpark on my ass an' wouldn't even let me borrow his pickup truck to ride to the hospital.

Estelle, my own Daddy's common-law wife's one drove me.

So, I don't see any future in actin' like a goll-durned Redskin or kickin' TVs.

I say, Hell! Let Elvis do it. An' I AIN'T ELVIS.

He takes a snort from a pint bottle.

So. Now. Lookin' out yonder to the Little Dickie, the Birthday Boy, an' his brand-new Birthday puppy, I got a idea I oughta dedicate my next number to the brand-new Birthday puppy, cause I gotta feelin' he's gonna identify with it. It's call, "Hey! Hey! I'm All Shook Up!"

An' I think y'all're gonna like it 'cause it's one of my all-time personal bigger fav'rites.

A hit in its own right.

But first I wanna take a little snort an' make a toast here to Little Dickie, the Birthday Boy, an' to all ah you,

An' hell, to me, too,

'cause . . .

I AIN'T ELVIS!

He drinks as lights dim out.

30

Calling Elvis

TIM J. LORD

Scene: Just outside a movie theatre in Memphis. On the marquee: "Naked Gun, Starring Leslie Nielsen and Priscilla Presley." A man, the Tracker, is standing against one of the walls of the cinema. He wears a trenchcoat, a T-shirt saying "50 million Elvis fans can't be wrong," and blue suede shoes. The man is scrutinously watching the people who enter the cinema.

THE TRACKER: No. No. No. Dammit! I know that he'll be here. How can he resist? It's the Memphis grand opening of his wife's film debut! I've been tracking him since the First Annual Impersonators' Convention in Las Vegas, and this has been my best lead yet. Oh yes! He'll be here. And I'll be the one to find him. It's all just a matter of perception—knowing the fakes from the genuine article. And knowing how to think like him. Think so much like him that I actually become him. Like that guy there! His mutton chops are a quarter of an inch too long. Or him. He's three and a half pounds too heavy. Wait a sec. Now here's a real possibility. No . . . No! Oh please! He's eating a veggie burger. The real man would never eat a veggie burger.

Oh, he's gotta be here! Somewhere! I mean he has to know what it feels like to be bound to someone but to be separated from that person for so many years. Someone you laughed with. Someone you shared your deepest secrets with. Someone who possibly knows you better than you know yourself. And this . . . this is his only chance to see that someone . . . to see the woman he loved (*The Tracker unconsciously pulls several photographs from an interior pocket of his trenchcoat and delivers the following lines to those photos*)—to really see her. Well, to see her as best as is possible under the circumstances. I mean, when you lose someone like that, someone who's a real part of you, how can you help but stumble around trying to get that person back once you realize what you've lost. At the very least, (*He looks up from the photos at last. Unconsciously, returns them to his pocket*) you have to find a replacement because sometimes you just can't have that person, so whether or not you realize that you can't have what you want, you look for someone, something, to fufill that . . . hole.

So, yeah, he's lost her and he wants her back. But he can't have her back, so he goes for the next best thing—a twenty-foot high projection of her. And you know that when the movie comes out on video he's gonna be the first to buy it so that he can watch her over and over without leaving the safety and comfort of his home and his anonymity.

(*Eyeing someone suspiciously*) Wait a minute! What about hi—? No. that's not him either. The problem here is that all these guys are too conspicuous. No, I need someone more subtle. Someone who wants to get into this movie so badly but is not interested in nor he is willing to draw attention to himself.

During the following description, the Tracker unconsciously finds himself becoming the very thing he's describing.

Someone who's alone. Darting, looks all about, but focused on achieving the door to the cinema. Once inside, he would cast a quick look back over his shoulder and then . . . move right to the snack counter. Disguising his voice, he would order a light snack: Large soda, hot dog, popcorn, Jujubes and probably some Junior Mints. The food purchased, he ascertains the precise location of the appropriate auditorium—probably the main one as it's opening night. The main auditorium . . . where there's more people to see him but, that being the case, it's easier for him to get lost in the crowd.

He enters. The previews have already begun because, naturally, he's waited till the last possible moment so that he can enter unseen in darkness. Now . . . for the selection of the seat—this is a crucial moment because he needs to have . . . an aisle seat close to a fire exit so that he can leave the building before everyone else—a very important, trademark characteristic. No impersonator would feel the need to go this far in a common movie theatre.

So, he scans the auditorium, knowing that he's only moments away from this long-awaited, long-cherished reunion. Knowing also that if he can't get precisely the right seat, he will have to abort his mission with only his Jujubes to comfort him. In fact, he's probably done his reconnaissance, coming to other opening nights of big films to find that perfect seat—films which he could walk out on with only his Jujubes and still feel all right.

So it's all down to whether or not that one seat—that one seat, which he scouted out months ago when he first learned of the impending release of her movie—whether or not that one seat is open, anxiously awaiting his arrival. That one seat that will allow him to see her in all her silver-screen glory and allow him to remain successfully anonymous.

His eyes have raised to look upon the screen; he's almost afraid to look at that one seat he has chosen for himself. Wanting so much to see her tonight, but afraid to be confronted with failure. Afraid to be confronted with the idea of waiting long months for the video release and afraid that for the first reunion he will have to settle for the twenty-inch version of his love instead of the all-embracing twenty feet.

But he's running out of time. The previews are coming to an end. He has to sit down before the movie starts or else when he attempts to sit, people will get annoyed. People will look. And then . . . they'll know. They'll see right through the nineteen years of absence, the nineteen years of anonymity. Be they fans or no, be they young or old, they will look and they will see; they will understand. And then all the fears and anxieties of the moment, all the years of confusion and doubt and shame will all come crashing down upon him and he will have no choice but to drop everything—even his precious Jujubes—and run! Run for the exit! Run for his life—the only bit of his life that he still has left: His nonexistence!

In fact! What time is it? Five past seven?! That's what he's doing now! To the fire exit!

He runs offstage in the direction of the fire exit. There is a pause and then suddenly a loud clatter as if someone has just been tackled and fallen into a bunch of trash cans.

(*From offstage*) Oh dear. I . . . I'm terribly sorry. I thought that you were someone else.

There is a sound as of someone being hit in the stomach and collapsing to the ground. In a moment, the Tracker stumbles back onstage, clutching his stomach.

Dammit. I thought for sure that I had him. I really thought that I was into his mind that time. That I'd gotten in touch with everything he was thinking, feeling, doing.

Ah, what am I doing here! What am I doing, period? I'm attempting to find a person who may or may not exist. But I'll never find him. He's always eluding me. All I ever succeed in finding is my own stupidity—the fact that I'm wrong once again. About him. About myself. About everything.

Why can't I find him? He and I are like this. (*Holding them up, he crosses his fingers*) We are one and the same, but he's always never where I think he should be.

I need a sign. An omen. An omen, God!!! Give me a sign that I should go on with my search!

He looks to the sky; there is no response. He hangs his head. A man enters, reading a newspaper and holding it so that his face is concealed. He stops, leans against one of the walls of the cinema.

Written in big headlines on the paper for all the world to see: "36 Hour Elvis Film Festival This Weekend!" The man with the newspaper coughs. The Tracker looks up, sees the headline. He goes closer to read the article. Whirls around.

That's it! How foolish of me. He wouldn't think of missing his own films! This whole Priscilla business was probably just a ploy to escape me. But not this time. Oh no. Now, it stretches out, all clear and plain before me. (*The Tracker whips out the photos of before and addresses the following to them*) I'll show you! This time I'll prove to you that I don't need you. I'm a free man! You hear? (*He throws the photos to the ground, considers spitting on them but reconsiders and uncomfortably swallows his spittle.*) Film Festival! Here I come. There is no escaping this time. This time, I am him. I know exactly what to do and where to go.

The Tracker runs offstage. There is a moment's hesitation and then the Tracker strolls back onstage, casually picks up the photos, and slips them back into his pocket before bolting off again. The man looks over his newspaper to see if he is gone. When certain of this, he folds up the paper, checks his watch, darts a few glances about, and hurries into the building looking once more over his shoulder before fully committing to the cinema. Then he is away to the snack counter.
Strangely, he bears an incredible resemblance to The King.

Private Elvis

LAVONNE MUELLER

SERGEANT SUGAR: I was company cook at Fort Hood when Elvis was a raw recruit. Yah, I saw him look like all the other guys. Crew cut. Fatigues. He use to polish his brass better than any of them. But what I remember best from those days was when Elvis pulled KP. That's right, he pulled Kitchen Police just like the rest.

He didn't ever want no special favors. I'm talking here about hard duty stuff—scrubbing pots and pans and scouring the grease trap. I've seen men who later won medals in Nam cry when they had to tackle the grease trap. These days grunts got it easy, with a lotta modern disposal equipment. But in them times, we had this contraption that looked like a little septic tank outside the kitchen that collected all the oily crude. It was a mean thing.

Later Elvis went into Special Services and had it soft. But first he had to go through Basic Training. There he was treated like an ordinary recruit. He actually liked it that way. Said for once he could give his pelvis a rest and even belch off-key. He didn't have to be professional for a while.

At that time when the King came through, I had just made sergeant with an MOS in baking. Everybody called me Sgt. Sugar 'cause I boiled my dumplings with a cup of sugar. My cabbage and beets, too. I got a sweet tooth. Never did get checked out on no rifle range. Me—I was checked out on a Coleman stove. I cooked so good the Company Commander never let me leave the mess hall. I was in Korea, but the only fighting I did was aimed at stomachs. Now a belly don't take sides. And it's got a mixture of hydrogen, carbon dioxide, and even methane. Every one of us is all walking explosions. Even

Elvis. Especially Elvis with the things he snorfed down. The way I figure it, good food is victory, and maybe I contributed to the only victory there was in what Truman had the nerve to call a Police Action. Well, I didn't see nobody over to Korea wearing little whistles around their neck. I seen me men with weapons around their neck.

Most of the time it was my duty to sit on a federal green stool near the stove drinking my own black gritty coffee and yelling out orders to the right and to the left of me. There's something beautiful and patriotic about a lot of shining pots hanging from the ceiling. I love to see steam coming up from a giant pan of boiling spuds—holds my attention.

Elvis and me hit it right off that day he pulled KP. Cause he liked my *cat heads*—those were the spoon biscuits I personally made for mess every Sunday morning. Light as Ping-Pong balls. I seen him eat fifteen to twenty at a sitting. Elvis liked fried Jell-O on his. Ate them two at a time. He said eating just one insulted his mama. Her biscuits were flatter than mine, but he could stack them better, was all that was.

Elvis also took to me seeing as how I was R.A.—Regular Army all the way. I'd been around. He said he respected experience. 'Cause I had seen things. Not like a lot of his hick cousins. Not that he didn't like his hick kin. He love them. But once in a while it was interesting to meet a man who'd traveled. Had adventures. Not adventures like he had— singing in halls and dives and cramped TV and radio stations. But foreign and exotic adventures. Like me cooking in the jungle alongside vultures who had them a seven-feet wingspan. Hell, in Ko-rea, parakeets sleep upside down. Guy quails sit on the eggs. Moths grow a foot wide. Spiders spin webs strong enough to knock your cap off. Elvis loved me telling him junk like that.

I also had a string of medals. Lotta times the mess got shelled in Korea. Guys who were gung-ho would panic with pork sausage and fried eggs in their mouth. They'd forget their helmet liners. I don't exactly know why that is. There would be hysteria and trampling you don't see on the battle-field. I'd end up protecting some dimwit by putting a skillet on his head. I saved a hell of a lot of men with pie tins.

That day Elvis come in to my mess to pull KP was a day I'm not ever gonna forget. It was raining, making it even steamier inside. Four in the morning, but he was perky. Helped hisself to a glass of milk. Never saw him drink much coffee. I could see he wanted me to treat him like anybody. He was working hard to act like anybody—yawning, scratch-ing his famous crotch, then stacking the metal trays right away and putting out the salt and pepper shakers on the long wooden tables even before I told him he had to. The two idiots with him, Private Odegaard and Private Sprague, kinda held back, just following Elvis around like *he* was suppose to give them orders—not me.

After breakfast, Elvis and his two buddies hit the dirty frying pans with gusto and scrubbed the floor. When my back was turned, them two dumb sidekicks tried to steal the mop Elvis used. Said they wanted to share it. I put a stop to that. No way was I gonna pay for any stolen inventory, be it monumental or not.

Lunch went fine. Elvis worked harder than the other two guys put together. But by dinner, the King was dragging. He was in good shape then, pretty muscular and not at all blub-bery like he got later. But I was working them three hard. Not any harder than usual, mind you. Just regular KP duties.

It was midnight and the three of them was finished in the kitchen. It was time to clean the grease trap. Steel wool was bunched up high along the floor like piles of stiff black flowers. I got myself a beer and told the guys to take a fifteen-minute break. Elvis instantly fell gracefully to the floor, full out on his back, spreading his rock and roll legs apart, closing his eyes. Odegaard and Sprague fell flat on their stomachs with a thud, sort of whining pitifully cause their hands were blistered.

Then, all of a sudden, Elvis says to me: "Sargeant Sugar, sing to me."

I said: "Elvis, I can't sing."

Elvis says: "Yes, you can. Cooking is the greatest kind of singing. Just reel off a list of your best dishes—ones you done here and around the world. That'll be all the music I wanna hear."

Sprague and Odegaard sat up when the King said that. They forgot their burning red hands.

I said: "Elvis, *me*? Singing for *you*?"

He said: "Yep."

So I took a gulp of beer, wrapped my legs around the stool, closed my eyes, and let a string of specialties float across my mind. I entered a near trance and half hummed and droned: "Easter egg bread . . . paper bag apple pie . . . pull and tuck rolls . . . ice cream peanut butter pie . . . Polish pickle soup . . . bedroll chicken . . . corn creole . . . line shack green chili . . . squaw pudding . . . chuck wagon grit stew . . . ohmygosh goulash . . ."

Then without any warning, Elvis jumped up and took his signature stance, thrusting out his lower body and pretending to strum a guitar. He sung to his own tune:

"Fried okra
cooter stew
porkettes
white gravy

hot potato salad
dirty rice

sauerkraut salad
yo yo puddin
oh, my, yo yo
baby my puddin

punch pie
punch
punch my heart pie

pear squash pickles
monkey bread rye
jam cake
jam my cake
jam
jam so much I could die."

Elvis fell gracefully back to the floor and closed his eyes again.

It was the best Elvis song I ever heard. It had soul. It had Baptist yearning—ceramic and crimson. It rocked with love and longing. Jesus was in it, too, along with his mama.

Odegaard and Sprague stared with their mouths open. They knew it was an experience they'd be telling family and friends for the rest of their lives.

It was 2 A.M. by the time the three of them finished cleaning the grease trap. They were all an oily mess as they headed back to the barracks.

Elvis never pulled no more KP. Usually guys got it three or four times in Basic Training. I guess he felt he had done his "just like anybody" duty. I did see him in the mess from time to time. We'd chat over my *cat heads* and I'd tell him about the time I fried an egg on a piece of paper in Korea, baked bread on a shovel, watched ants over there eat the little blue veins outta Roquefort cheese, how I bunked at night on a bed of jungle orchids, the usual stuff. Once he even asked me if I'd work for him after he got discharged. But I'm Regular Army and it's hard for me to think of myself anywhere but in the Service. Besides, dump me into civilian life, and I'm just Joe Smuck. Here to the Army, I'm Sergeant Sugar. Then, too, if I went with Elvis and he got tired of my singing, I'd be like a lotta guys I know—selling stuff from an aluminum suitcase on State Street.

Nobody ever mentioned that song he sang on KP. Not me. Not Odegaard or Sprague though them two bums did steal the mop Elvis used and axed it fair and square right through the center of the handle, on down to even dividing the braided soapy rags like two scalps. I held their bacon and jerky till they paid up for it. But I didn't have the heart to be harboring bad feelings 'cause the music Elvis sung that night still lingers on me like a light dusting of baking powder. I've kept up with the King's career over the years, and I ain't never heard anything he's done as good as he done that.

A Pair of Eyes

JUDY GeBAUER

Terry is a middle-aged woman with dyed red hair, which she styles in a sixties bouffant. She is a waitress in a diner catering to truckers. She is in the diner now, about to close, cleaning the counter.

TERRY: He worked at it, you mind.
You bet he worked at it.
But he already had something to work with.
Mainly he had the eyes.
I'd never married Buddy
if it wasn't for those eyes.
I don't admit that to myself
but truth to tell
I'd never noticed him
but for that.
Oh he's a good lookin' fella back then,
Buddy, I mean,
nice body and all,
back then,
but lots of boys come in the diner
lookin' good and lookin' lonely,
just off the turnpike,
nice bodies on 'em.
Buddy, I just couldn't get over the eyes.
You remember them deep dark eyes of Elvis?
Melt you right down to goo.
Buddy'd strut in the diner,
park his rig outside there in the lot,
then strut in the far door there

so he could walk the whole length of the dining room,
that belt buckle,
that black hair careful combed,
growed long on the sides,
the eyes dark, kind of soft cruel sweet,
sat him down at the counter right here,
here's Buddy's old stool,
had that nice lean stomach back then,
that thick belt with the studs
just as tight on him as he could stand it,
could hardly draw a breath,
could hardly even sit the stool,
his jeans was just painted on him.
Then the fool'd sit here,
eat him a bowl of chili or two.
I must have served him a ton of chili,
lots of meat, lots of sauce,
he'd sit here and eat the chili deluxe
all night long,
and that's the double portion,
extra size bowls,
just so he could hear people say,
"That fella could be his twin, bless his dear heart,"
or "I bet he's good to his mother,
that fella eatin' the chili there,
looks so much like the King";
that sort of comment;
or "You with the band, son?"
or one old woman said,
"Are you him? I won't bother you. Just are you him?"
Buddy's way was just let them dark eyes of his
rest on the person,
just smile at 'em, shy, don't say.
Don't say one way or the other.
Let 'em believe.
He always says to me,

"Honey, people gotta believe
in somethin'.
They gotta feel special."
I think he mighta been talkin'
about his own self,
you know,
now I think about it,
I think Buddy really needed to feel
like he was a special man,
doin' a special thing for people.

Maybe if it was crowded
Buddy'd order him a chicken fried steak,
some home fries,
collard greens,
all on top of that chili deluxe,
sometimes a piece of pie even,
don't know how he stood
that belt so tight,
all them dinners
one on top of the other.
He'd take a break when I took my break.
Meet me out the back there.
Caught him loosening that belt a notch once or twice.
But he'd keep on with Elvis,
the way he thought Elvis was with women,
even when he was out the back there alone with just me,
and his belt loosed a couple notches,
that smile,
kind of like his feelings been hurt,
kind of like he's so glad to see you
he can't quite show it,
them eyes,
never talking much to me except
"Please, ma'am, can I kiss you?,"
like he guessed Elvis would say it.

We all knew how polite a young man
Elvis was,
even when he got great,
very polite to his fans,
and Buddy tried to emulate that politeness.

Well, sir, I mean to say,
when Elvis went in the army,
I guess Buddy went in the army.
I guess a lotta boys thought,
hey, if the King goes, I go.
Buddy served.
Yes indeed.

Later,
we'd been married a couple years maybe,
I got up the courage to ask him,
"How come me? Why'd you marry me?"
We was havin' a little time,
Buddy and me,
just not quite settlin' into bein'
married.
I wondered sometimes why Buddy bothered with me.
Buddy says,
"You'd have been his choice."
"What about me would he like so much?"
"Ah, Terry, why all about you. Your hair.
He's crazy about redheads."
I never asked Buddy but I should've,
"How about you,
you crazy about redheads?
You sure don't act much like it."
Well, these days now
I get to wonderin',
Buddy on the road most of the time,
did he ever love me?

Me. Terry.
Or did he just want what he guessed
Elvis would want?
Elvis wouldn't look twice at me.
That's for darn sure.
Be polite to me, but he wouldn't look twice.

All them burgers and shakes and chili
caught up with Buddy,
he just got that belly now,
why hardly a belt will fit around him.
He still keeps his belt pulled tight
over that gut.
Makes him look more like a gnome
with a seed cap on than the rock star
he used to look like.
He says, well, the Man himself
put on a little weight later on, too.

She puts away her rag; takes off her apron.

And my goodness,
look at me,
cookin' for Buddy,
workin' here all these years,
I don't know where my figure went,

but the eyes,
Buddy's still got them dream eyes,
remember how soft and deep
Elvis' eyes could get
when he sang the ballads?

When he sang the ballads.

Why's all the good people go young?

Why isn't bein' married like a ballad?

I married Buddy's eyes,
to be close to Elvis,
to pay him some homage,
to lie with a man
with deep soft eyes.

I married a pair of eyes
and Buddy married a hair-do.

She hangs up a Closed sign.

Chasing a Dream

DAVID AND CAROL HEGBERG

It was 1963, and high school was a drag. We were bored to death of homework and tired of the long winter. We needed a break, both mentally and physically. The basketball season wasn't going all that well, Christmas vacation had passed, and most of us were looking for something interesting to do. If it had been summer, we'd have taken the train to a Cubs game. To make matters worse, it wasn't that long since the President had been shot in Dallas. It seemed like everyone was down in the spirit.

Dale came into the classroom, excited about something. He was actually drawing a crowd, even though he wasn't a popular guy. But he was a good friend of mine. I strolled over to see what was up. He held a *Rockford Star* newspaper ad that said an Elvis concert was scheduled at the University of Wisconsin, Madison, the next weekend.

"Well," I said, "at least it was something to think about besides homework."

"Maybe we could go up and try to get tickets," Dale suggested. "At least get a glimpse of the King of rock and roll."

The more I thought about it, the more I liked the idea. The rest of the week seemed to never end.

Finally Saturday we took off in Dale's dad's car, headed toward Wisconsin in twenty-degree weather. We arrived early in the afternoon to find the college auditorium. (We had a time trying to park.) At the ticket office, we were told they were sold out. What a disappointment!

We decided to get something to eat, then see a show. The restaurant was at least warm and the food decent. In the booth beside us, I overheard someone talking about Elvis. I told Dale to hush so I could hear. They said Elvis was staying at a private residence. With relatives. (I thought the King came from the South. But he could have relatives in the North.) These relatives lived on Lighthouse Road, the third farmhouse on the right after leaving Route 14.

After we left the restaurant, Dale was all bent out of shape about not getting tickets. I told him since we knew where Elvis would be staying, maybe we could sneak a peak at him after the concert. Dale's eyes lit up like a beacon.

The show got out about 9:30, and we drove around a while, then headed for Lighthouse Road. Dale started getting second thoughts about snooping in a dark area we didn't know. He was the one who wanted to drive to Wisconsin, I reminded him. Then I called him chicken a couple of times, and that didn't help any. But I wouldn't be denied my chance to see Elvis.

We parked near the second farmhouse. As I got out of the car, Dale said he couldn't leave his old man's car alone. "It's my responsibility," he kept saying. I almost begged him but finally whispered under my breath, "Oh, what the hell. Stay here, you little coward," and left.

This was the biggest adventure of my life, and even though I was scared, I was going through with it. As I crept toward the third farmhouse, I hoped no farm dogs were out. I really wanted to see Elvis drive through the front gate and walk in the house.

In the distance I could see dim lights and crept across the snowy field toward them. I tried to make no noise. It's always good to let sleeping dogs lie, especially if you really don't belong there! I ran into a barbed wire fence and tore my coat sleeve. Once over that, it was easygoing, even in the dark.

I eased my way up to a window. It was an old-fashioned living room. All old furniture. Lots of books lined one wall, but no TV. I saw an old lady knitting in a rocking chair.

Then I heard some one behind say, "Freeze and turn around slowly."

There stood an old codger, holding a shotgun straight at me.

All I could say was "Don't be cruel," in my joking way.

The old man let out a long sigh. "Darned young kids today!"

"I didn't mean any harm, sir," I said, trying to be real polite.

"I'm sure you didn't. Just like those others who stomped through Ma's honeysuckle." He looked me over good in the light from the window. "I suppose you came to see Elvis," he almost shouted.

"Well, . . . sir . . ." I stammered. How could I convince him I wanted to more than life itself?

Before I could say more, he marched me inside, shoved on by his shotgun.

Inside was warm and cozy with the smell of good cooking still lingering. The gray-haired woman walked into the kitchen. "Found another one, huh, Pa?" Then she giggled like a schoolgirl.

The old man stood his shotgun in the corner. As he walked to the table, he muttered, "Wasn't loaded anyway." He was a tough-looking old duffer. I guess he could rely on that out here in the sticks. "Make some hot cocoa, Ma. For the young 'un. I'll take coffee."

Immediately she went to work, laughing under her breath.

"Sit down," he commanded. And I did. "Now tell me. Who is this . . . Elvis?"

I couldn't believe that statement. Those darn restaurant kids had led us on a goose chase. So I sat down and drank hot chocolate and told them the story of the King.

Arianne

CRAIG FOLS

Arianne, a young woman

ARIANNE: America gets these crazy ideas into its head. Every hundred years or so, like, Let's Kill All the Indians. Let's murder the buffalo and leave their carcasses on the ground to rot. Let's cut out their tongues and leave the rest of them on the prairie to decompose. So the birds can gnaw out their eyes or something. Waste them.

Or Vietnam. I have a good idea. Let's go into Asia, and get those nasty little gooks in line. Let's enter the jungle, and mow it down. Let's invade what is essentially an agrarian economy and introduce devastation the likes of which humanity has never seen. That'll make the world a better place.

Or Nixon. What a nice man.

Or segregation. Yeah, that'll work.

And then of course things turn. People change their minds, after everything is ruined and it's too late anyway. Reality is revealed to be different from what it was, and we all want to be Kevin Costner, dancing around with his butt hanging out.

It's like Elvis. What the fuck was that about?

My Bonny Elvis

MAUREEN McCOY

Thin light-skinned woman, 50, wearing calf-length skirt stands in small shadowy Edinburgh tourist shop room. As she begins to speak, she is touching a man's kilt, which is draped on a stand; she is half-hidden. A white handkerchief, framed, is on the wall. Also, a print of a kilted man.

So here you come, an American detective lad wanting to know if it's true, what they say in a book. Aye, someone finally told. Go on, then, look at the kilt until you cannae look no more. You've jolted a woman from her dream. Now what are you going to do with her? (*Steps more fully from behind the kilt, still clutches it*) No touching. No snapshots. Pictures cannae hold a miracle.

You're right that Elvis never toured outside the U.S. His Colonel Parker was an illegal, dinnae you know? and they would have snatched him up in a minute. His Colonel ruled like God: he couldnae leave Elvis, so—Jack Sprat—Elvis couldnae leave America.

How did Elvis get to Em'bur then? Same as any country boy, he ran away. After one wee nag of a day, Elvis put the Colonel down with pills, and when they took effect he boinged his finger onto a spinning globe and stopped the world at Scotland. "Boys," he said, "we're flyin' out while the Colonel takes his nap."

Mr. Smith always handled the gents, but just like the Colonel, that day Mr. Smith was out of the game. I'd convinced him, "Go walk the Pentlands. You've a fine day for it." Fridays are slow on the Royal Mile, all the tours heading up the highlands. Mind, one day without Mr. Smith's nose hairs to look at would be relief enough. I dinnae expect anything more than that to happen, I dinnae think of stars and dreamlife.

Aye, the shop looked like this except for the computer contraptions—clan software that flashes history and tartans at the push of a button—and it smelled just the same. Mr. Smith has never noticed I've changed nothing, ever. These are exactly the floorboards Elvis walked.

When Elvis came in the shop I dinnae recognize him right off. I thought, Here's another big beef of an American looking for a St. Andrew's scarf, or claiming a family hero. The lads had put him in tourist clothes: shiny white belt girded around his middle, sailboats on his dark navy shirt, and shoes of a color that screamed *Yank*.

Dinnae you know, I remember everything. I was wearing the McLean that day, wool in summer, but that's part of the job, and our summers can be anything: plenty of light but you never know what's behind it either. If a miracle is going to happen in Em'bur, summer is the time.

One of his lads told me later, aside, that Elvis "freaked out" once they had left the Colonel behind. The lads did what they could on the plane ride coming over, to divert Elvis from his jitters. They dunked his head in red hair dye, one of them thinking in advance to what Elvis would want in Scotland: disguise. McElvis, they called him. The MacEee. They bushed out his hair with a dryer and spray—(*She makes great tugging, hair-teasing, twisting and spraying motions, circling the imaginary seated Elvis*)—and when Elvis came through that door, his buggerish boys surrounding him and keeping guard in order to put off any other shoppers, dinnae you know he looked like an upright savage boar, what you'd imagine of the one whose tooth they keep down at Holyroodhouse, still, as proof that the beast once had the gall to attack a royal. They keep the tooth in the room next to Mary Queen of Scots, with the fake blood painted on the floorboards. Blood from hundreds of years back; we dinnae like to forget anything. It is in my bones to forget nothing. And Holyroodhouse is what the lads had noticed, driving in, Elvis all excited to see how real royalty lived. But he turned peckish on hearing that our palace had nearly three hundred rooms to Graceland's wee twenty-three. The lads hurried him on up the Royal Mile, shoppers' row, to distract Elvis.

Fate, there stood I.

Actor becomes Elvis. Walks through shop door, soft bell tingling.

"I'm sweatin like a hog. These pants are ridin' up my crack somethin' fierce. I'm in desperate need. Hey, can you help me, little mama? Help me."

His discomfort was real, but what was occurring to Elvis even as he complained, was the possibility of freedom. Imagine it: He hadnae ken freedom since childhood, and he stood there, the biggest boy of them all, ready. He was looking at kilts, Elvis was. Kilt salvation, a whole new kind, was what he could see.

Actor becomes Elvis.

"Yeah, kilt me up, mama, or I'm a split somethin' here quick."

My cheeks were burning.

I explained before we got started that a kilt is not a costume. You dinnae ever wear a kilt to masquerade balls or to your rodeos over there. Kilts are dress-up.

Actor becomes Elvis.

"All them palace guardses got 'em on." Elvis spoke in a child's voice, a pout.

I explained, further, that the tourist industry counted as dress-up, that we considered the offering of hospitality as a wee grave gift of ourselves. Aye we do, Scots. Stationing kilted men at our points of interest sets a tone.

Actor becomes Elvis.

"Pretty mama, I want one, hear? Kilt me up cool. I want to walk in a kilt and be nobody's business at all."

No one had ever called me pretty. No one had ever spoken to me in a crooner's voice. I remember it like yesterday, of course I do. Elvis stood right over there. His lads crowded the doorway, eyes in all directions. One of them kept flicking at the hems of kilts lined against the wall. They wouldnae have slept in ages. I told them expect to see daylight until eleven o'clock, then watch it come back at four in the morning. I spoke as carefully as I could, as I had trained myself to do with Americans.

Actor becomes Elvis.

"Yessir, there ain't no hidin in Jesus's heaven. He's a-shinin' sun down on me non-stop, boys, but I'm a trick folks now, with the help of little mama."

Every time he said that, *little mama*, I went meek and staunch and heartbroken as some Jane Eyre. I could fix him up. I could make Elvis, of the wild-boar red hair, look more Scottish and true on the Royal Mile than anything he'd ever dreamed of. I could love Elvis.

Of course I remember the wee detail. This is when time stopped and dreamlife took over. Twenty-five years ago, Elvis coming in the shop was all that had ever happened to me. I cannae deny it. Sorry, I mean to talk only in my tourist English. I am educated, but when the heart gets talking we go back to being our natural fool selves. My heart is talking and hurting and wanting still to dream. I am breaking apart, coming forward like this, though I am noble, aye, very noble to do so. I am stepping out of the dream of my life. (*She lets go of the kilt*) I have dreamed my whole adult life, from then until now. What happens next? What becomes of people who are struck by lightning and left to wander? (*She stands still, in front of the kilt*)

A beat. Actor becomes Elvis.

"Can you suit me up right quick? How does the kilt thing-a-ding work?"

I told Elvis I could kilt him up smartly, and then—think of the future—we could design a special tartan, if he wanted that. It is not illegal to add a tartan to the bunch as long as you register it with the Office of the Lord Lyon. The Presley tartan. I was already picturing something red: a relative of royal Stewart, with the yellows and blacks gone wild as lightning. Maybe throw in some deep streaking greens. Youth! I actually considered what fame would be, as the designer of the Presley tartan.

Yanks come in off the street impatient. They catch the kilt lust, usually after a pub crawl, and some cannae possibly wait for special orders. They'll wear any old tartan, never mind whose clan, and that is especially brilliant if they lack Scottish blood altogether. It borders on costuming, but we can only warn what is correct. We do not cross the water and watch the circumstances under which they wear the kilts. So with American impatience and American girth in mind, we keep ready-mades, some run-up kilts in stock. I prayed to our first saint, Columba, that I could fit Elvis in a kilt. Let our biggest kilt work—the sumo you'll want to call it—hanging across the back room like a banquet of itself.

I brought out this kilt. Look at it. (*She fans the kilt*) Unfurled, it's as wide as Holyrood's dining table is long. Isle of Skye, 'tis. This kilt, I can tell you, weighs half a stone, but they say—I've read, read everything since—that his belt buckles were twice that heavy in silver and gold.

I prayed further. Please let the length be right: one inch above the knee. Because you dinnae hem a kilt. Never do you hem a kilt. The kilt falls to the selvege or nothing. Our kilt makers are trained for five years to be able to cut for length and fit. It's only the ladies' kilt skirts you see hemmed, up and down the street—mostly cheap blends too. No, there is nothing like a man's kilt for heft and serious beauty. I was twenty-five and very, very serious. I was twenty-five and shy, twenty-five and facing Elvis who, now with the shop door locked, and backed into the dressing room with only the curtain around him, wanted to try on his kilt. Elvis' zeal made him stomp and snort, and that red hair was shot out like flame.

I got the kilt loosely put around Elvis, without having to see anything embarrassing, and then he emerged. I am telling you that our one giant of a kilt that we'd kept back for an age now, stood us the trick. There ya be: Highland Elvis. Bonny Highland Elvis.

Actor becomes Elvis. He poses left and right in the mirror. Speaks to his image.

"Hey, y'all. Hi, stranger."
Like the cinema cowboys. He liked calling himself that. Stranger. I told him I had to measure length. We just had to make sure. Hold still, heh, heh, I said.
Then, trembling, I was crouched before Elvis (*she crouches before the kilt*) and there—God's truth—I realized I was facing something the planet Earth had never seen: Elvis' knees, twin white worlds of such giant proportions I had the unnatural desire to measure them. I was in a fairy story now. I kneeled there, staring, my hand high and gripping the wool of the kilt as if I had business doing so. I hung on—yes I remember everything! His one knee was unaccountably sooty. Elvis' handkerchief fluttered down at me, like a parachute. There, I said. There, pressing the cloth to his great knee.
(*Beat*) I understood, of course, that the Elvis knees, as *Elvis* knees, had no place in the public eye, none at all. I was at a private viewing. He acknowledged my shock and the intimacy.

Actor becomes Elvis.

"Go ahead, little mama. Kiss it. That's all right, pretty mama. Kiss it."

I kissed him. Right there in the great dimple of the great bouldered knee.

Me lips were humming, and already he was stepping past me.

Actor becomes Elvis.

"Boys, I kin just feel what a highland warrior I'd be. I kin feel it."

Wobble-brained, I rose and busied myself in the jackets. (*She rises, turns away*) Elvis had kept his shirt on, an openneck thing mad with those sailboats. I gave him a white blouse and day jacket. (*She holds up clothing*) These go with your kilt, I told him. Try these. I was babbling the kilt words like love: argyll, sporran and chain, flashes, hose, belt.

One of the lads took me aside while Elvis outfitted his upper body.

Actor becomes swaggering sidekick.

"Good gull. Thankee. This is calmin' him. You know yer stuff." I ignored his lewd wink but blushed. He kept on: "I seen you kneelin' before the King. You was a plaid pleat away from his privates. What do you think of that?"

I went robotic. I recited lines of truth from the standard kilt book: *Only three occasions allow that a man wear something under his kilt: dancing, war, and parades.* And then I blurted, my voice a demon girl's: *Tell him so he'll be. . . correct!*

Actor becomes swaggering sidekick.

"Oh, sister, sister, sister!" This boy-man slapped me on the back. "Yer a rich little sister!"

Actor becomes Elvis.

"What're y'all doin ther with little mama? Behave yourself, bubs. We'se goin' for a stroll now. Aye, aye. Let me get some of them socks on. Hosiery? Little mama calls it hosiery! And that little purse thing? Fine, just fix me up to look like him." (*Elvis points to a print on the wall*)

A Highlander in dress, decked out in balmoral tam and dirk, you see. I advised Elvis against head gear and weapons. I presented him with hosiery. You want to cuff them, I told him. His own shoes would have to do. And those knees were shining like the white moons of love.

Elvis, as a red-headed boar, went oot the shop with his entourage. I saw them to the door and watched. There he went, striding up the Canongate like a bairn gone off to his first day of school. The lads aped along. Who could resist? I followed, though lagging. I saw the miracle unfold, and no one can take this beauty from me. Every time a stranger looked or nodded at Elvis, he dinnae see nothing but a Scot, a burly Scot oot on his business, looking like dignity and grace. You could see freedom hitting Elvis like a rare full Em'bur sun. What life might be, kilted, away from the Colonel and American need! I was proud of my countrymen, none of whom recognized Elvis. And Elvis turned his face up to the sky, to his Jesus, and seemed to thank the clouds which we always have plenty of. And the way Elvis walked he put a great swish to his kilt.

The only advice I'd given him was, Stay oot of the pubs. Forget Deacon Brodie's. You'll give yourself away.

All up the Canongate Elvis tried various poses and looked in windows, admiring himself more than the goods. Often enough he touched his bare knees. He kept looking around, watching all the people who dinnae know he was Elvis. Possibilities must have reeled in his mind. He seemed to take up more space than before, the whole world making way like a simple new friend.

When I saw the lads turning around I hurried back to my shop and they found me standing, as in the first instance, before the counter. The smell of wool, which was usually so dull, now wildly drugged my mind.

Actor becomes Elvis, comes in shop subdued, patting down his pleats like a schoolgirl.

"It's somethin'. It's a spiritual experience. I am completely unknown in this here rig. I could do battle. I could see the sights. I could be anyone."

And aye, coming at you down a glen, or over the moors, this fire-head Elvis could thrillingly look like murder.

I wanted to say, Rot, rot, Ah know wot ye mean. Elvis, Ah really do.

Elvis was silent then behind the curtain, taking off the kilt. One of his lads paid in full, wads of sterling, nearer to one thousand U.S. than not, while Elvis stood holding his kilt, taking a gander at the print on the wall. It was an original R. R. MacIan. Mr. Smith had impressed this on me. It would never be for sale.

The lads were buying up little tourist things out of the window: toffees and plaid pens and clan key fobs with their Latin mottos. They wiped out the whole display of whiskey-flavored fudge.

Actor becomes Elvis.

"Can't take back nothin' too noticeable."

I nodded. His knees were covered in tourist trousers again. His knees were luminous, anyway, and forever in my mind.

Actor becomes Elvis.

"Here, pretty mama." He was handing me the kilt.

But it was all paid for, I said. I dinnae understand.

Actor becomes Elvis.

"Can't take it with me. Can't give myself away now, can I?"

(*Takes kilt off stand*) Aye, I told him, but not too convincingly. I stood there holding the kilt.

Actor becomes Elvis.

"Keep it safe for me, mama. This here's a heaven I've found me. I'm a come back, hear. You gonna take care of the Elvis kilt for me, little mama? You gonna be here to dress me up when I come back?"

Aye, went my whisper. Oh, aye.

Actor becomes Elvis.

"This here's our secret, don't tell a soul. I'm a drop in out of the sky some day. My sweet Christ. You gonna be ready? Shhh, little mama. Shhhh." His finger ticking before my lips.

Gone then, Elvis and his lads were gone. I was left holding the folded kilt. I stood there forever. I held the kilt, a widow with the flag. . . . This is me. I put my face in it. I remembered the handkerchief and picked it up. The impression had settled. You see, I keep it under glass: the perfect face of the Elvis knee.

He never came back to me, not in the flesh.

I have been stunned faithful by Elvis, spun into a dream beyond what I could have ever hoped for here on the Canongate. If my dream has excluded the men who populate this earth, if it has excluded the life that comes with choosing one such man, that is the power of dream. Appearance cannae make anyone real. Invisibility assures eternal beauty. God wouldnae hardly deny it or He'd be denying Himself, now wouldnae He?

One o'clock. See here it is, the hour of his departure. Away with you, or watch: I cannae help it if you're still looking, it's what I do now, my dinner hour, but I'm usually in the back room, Mr. Smith out here with the gents.

Lights are dimming.

(*Beat*) I shed my clothes. (*Beat*) I take his kilt. (*Beat*) I lie down in it, rough wool, rolling me tight. (*Hugs kilt to her*) I am naked in the Elvis kilt, what he gie to me to dream, dark and wild in here, like heaven or like love. One hour, aye, my life.

Elvis' Last Supper

STEVE FEFFER

*Myra is a woman in her late sixties. She is dressed for the heat of
Las Vegas.*

MYRA: Dear Son: I was deeply disturbed to receive in the mail
your most recent correspondence. Why you sent me a packet
of brochures of various "retirement communities" is beyond
me. From the beginning you've been opposed to my move to
Las Vegas and your efforts in regards to arranging for me to
move back to Chicago or—God forbid—Miami Beach are
not only misspent, but compassionless. Perhaps if you would
take the time to visit me down here in my desert oasis, you
would see that not only am I doing well—I'm thriving!

For instance, I was deeply saddened that you were unable
to make it for Passover this year, the first I have not spent
with you in as long as I can remember. You won't believe who
came to my Passover Seder: Sylvia Handleman. That's right.
My friend Sylvia from the old neighborhood. She and her
husband Saul were down here for a linoleum tile convention.
What a treat that was for me.

Oh, yes. I almost forgot. And Elvis Presley was there too.
That's right. *The* Elvis Presley. Now that's a Seder. Elvis and
Sylvia Handleman. And you wanna put me in a home?

Perhaps I should explain. As you know, one of the plea-
sures I am enjoying most about Vegas is that there is no
shortage of entertainment. When you had me stuck in Miami
Beach, the highlight of the day was making it to the local
Friendly's in time for the Early Bird Special. Oh, no. Not
here. I go to all the shows. You know, the show lounges have
AARP specials. You wouldn't think so, but they do. I guess

63

that's because so many of the entertainers are my age. At any rate, I went to see Mr. Presley perform. He was . . . "feh." Something for the younger crowd, I suppose. But afterward, as I always do, I went to the back of the stage to get his autograph. I get 'em all. Deano. Sammy. Steve and Edie. I guess they let me go back because I look harmless. Good thing they don't talk to that-wife-of-yours, huh? Ha ha. Anyway, trust me: These autographs'll be worth something someday. They're part of your inheritance.

So I get to the back of the stage, and I can't even see Elvis. He's surrounded by what must be a hundred people, and I have to push my way to the front. And believe me, no one was letting me through because I was elderly. Picture the smoked fish counter at Zabar's on the eve of the high holidays and you get an idea of the scene. So I push back. In spite of what you and that-wife-of-yours-think, I can hold my own, and I finally get up to Elvis. And let me tell you something—he looked horrible. You don't really see it when he's up on that stage shaking his *tuchus*, and the lights are going, and it's glitz and glamour. But backstage, wearing a satin robe and sitting on a big lounger, with a TV tray resting on his huge belly piled high with fried chicken and some other kinda *shmutz*—well, picture your father right before the heart attack. May he rest in peace.

So he signs my program without even looking up from his meal. I mean, he gets chicken *schmaltz* all over it and everything. And I'm thinking, you know, someone oughtta say something to this man before he kills himself, and if I don't who will? I mean, you know I'm not one to hold my tongue. That may offend some—including that-wife-of-yours who doesn't know from a clean house or speaking up for herself because of her non-Jewish upbringing—but, hey, that's who I am. So I say to him, excuse me, Mr. Presley, when's the last time you had a decent meal? And Elvis finally looks up and says to me, 'scuse me ma'am? Look at that crap-ola in front of you, I say. When's the last time you had a decent meal? This is Southern goodness, he tells me. Southern goodness? What would your mother say if she saw you eating like that. Look, I'm having a few people over for the first Seder—Passover, you know, and why don't you come by. Seder? Passover? He looks all bewildered and his manager is trying to hurry me out of there. But as I resist his strong arm tactics I explain: It's the Jewish holiday celebrating the freedom from Egypt. You know, *The Ten Commandments*, Charlton Heston and all that. Still he doesn't understand. And so I say, you know, Jesus and the Last Supper; that was a Passover Seder. Well, that, of course, rang a bell in his *goyische* brain. The Last Supper he knows and now he's thinking out loud. Jesus attended a Seder; Elvis oughtta attend a Seder. If it's good enough for Jesus, it's good enough for Elvis. So, he told me to write down my address and hand it to his manager. I write down five o'clock and explain that we tell the whole story of Pesach with all the *baruchs* and what-nots, which he won't wanna miss, particularly since Saul Handleman is going to be there and even though he's a tile salesman he sings like an angel. In fact, Saul was going to be a Cantor, but his father convinced him to be a tile salesman. You know kinda like the Jazz Singer only with linoleum instead of jazz.

I set five places around my table. One for me, two for the Handlemans, and one for Elvis and whoever might join him. I'm thinking a man like Elvis probably can't go too many places by himself. The Handlemans arrived first. I explained who was going to be joining us and Sylvia looked a little disturbed. I guess she thought it was just going to be three of us. I mean you know how that Sylvia is. She always was very jealous of the time she spent with me. It was like that in old neighborhood. When I started dating your father, she was always trying to tag along. She and Saul kept on asking "how I was." You know, like they didn't believe me or something. And then she seemed very interested in whether or not I had talked to you lately and if you knew Elvis was going to be at the Seder. Like she's the only one who talks to her son—the big shot lawyer. Then she looked very pale and excused herself to go to the bathroom. That must've been when she left that hysterical phone message at your house with the baby-sitter.

Anyway, five o'clock rolls around and no Elvis. Five thirty—still no Elvis. Six, well, Sylvia and Saul are looking at their watches and I suggest we begin. Perhaps Elvis didn't understand what the whole thing was about. Perhaps he felt he didn't need to be there for the prayers and the story. You know, like your father. But I'm guessing Elvis doesn't miss too many meals and I just know that he'll be there in time for the brisket. Meanwhile, Sylvia and Saul were having a hard time concentrating on the Seder. They kept glancing at the empty place setting and then glaring at me. They tried to race through the whole Haggadah. Saul barely raised his voice once to sing. But I wouldn't let them. I'm not the most religious person, but the Pesach is one I take seriously. Our family overcame some hard times to be at the Seder table each year. It's a responsibility. So, finally we come to the four questions. Sylvia is ready to begin, but I stop her. I suggest we wait for Elvis to do it since he is the youngest and he might get a kick out of it. And that's when Sylvia really lets me have it. That's when she said that you were going to get an earful when she got back to Chicago. I had obviously lost my mind amidst all the noise and neon of Vegas. She damn near ruined the whole Seder.

Well, we spent the rest of the meal in the silence. We ate—I mean, God forbid Syl should miss a meal—but we didn't speak. In fact, we hardly exchanged a word until it came time to open the door to let Elijah in. Sylvia said that if I opened that door in this city of crooks and swindlers, that she was going to walk right out of it. Well, I wasn't going to let her do that. The setting of the cup for Elijah is my favorite part of the Pesach meal. It was always so mysterious for me as a little girl. My grandfather—your great grandfather—used to pour the cup of wine and then let me open the door. Then he'd start singing in his deep voice (*Singing*) "Eli-yah-hoo

Han-a-vee. Eli-yah-hoo Han-a-vee." Elijah the Prophet. And I would stare down the hall looking for him. And then, when I would turn back, the cup would be empty. Of course, later—when I was a big girl—I would turn around and know why his lips were red and he was laughing so hearty, but that moment never failed to enchant me. So I told Sylvia and Saul they could leave if they wanted to, but I was pouring that damn cup and opening my damn door and singing of Elijah the Prophet. And as I did I heard a loud clatter at the bottom of the stairs.

Well, first a man in a black suit entered and gave the place the once over. This got Syl and Saul off the couch. And then he was there. Not in a white suit like I sorta expected, but in a sport shirt and slacks. His hat in his hand. Real gentleman like. Sorry I'm late, ma'am, he said. I hope I didn't hold up your dinner. Nothing holds up our dinner, I told him; we're Jews.

Elvis sat down. His bodyguard sat down. And they listened while we finished reciting the blessings. His only sound was a loud "yahoo" as we all drank the fourth cup of wine—his first, or course. Well, at least his first at our table. I gathered he had a few glasses on his own prior to our Seder. I don't know, maybe he was at another Seder first. And then I served him his meal. He took a particular liking to the brisket and the Matzo balls. Though he didn't think much of the Matzo. You couldn't "sup up the beef juices like he did with a thick piece of his mama's corn bread," he said.

And then I asked him if he'd like to ask the four questions. He read those ancient words with a Southern accent that made it seem as if I was hearing them for the first time. "Why is this night different than all other nights?" Well, we all just looked around the table and laughed and laughed. We knew why it was different. We laughed until Saul—who obviously wanted to show off for Elvis—began to sing those questions in the most beautiful cantillation you've ever heard since Jan Peerce sang on the Lower East Side.

And when it came time to finish the closing songs. Elvis asked if he could sing one of his favorites. He said that he didn't know if it was right for the occasion, but it was one that he always sang in church, and it sure as heck reminded him of freedom. And I said to him, whatever he wanted to sing was fine with us. We were just glad to have him. And, oy, if that boy didn't sing the most gorgeous "Amazing Grace"—to die for it was. Not one of the five of us didn't have a tear in the eye. And before I could get him to sign his yarmulke for you, Son, he thanked me for a wonderful night, grabbed the half-filled bottle of Manischewitz, and he and his bodyguard were out the door.

So, as I said, Son, I don't know why you're sending me those brochures. I mean, unless, of course you have one for the Heartbreak Hotel. Ha ha. Things couldn't be better here, and you really are missing quite a time by choosing not to come down and see your old Mom. Perhaps you'll consider making it for Rosh Hashanah. I'm having my old friend Miriam Rabinowitz. You know Miriam from the old neighborhood. Oh, and Frank Sinatra is going to be there. Love. Mom.

Blue Christmas

LAURA QUINN

A living room in The Elvis Believer's home. A Christmas tree, totally done in Elvis, can be real or imagined. The Elvis Believer is talking to a first-time guest.

THE ELVIS BELIEVER: Oh, the tree. It's my Elvis tree. I used to have a normal Christmas tree, but that changed after I went to Graceland. I didn't buy anything at Graceland. I took the tour. I took pictures. I got a little misty at the grave. That's it. I went on a lark with a bunch of friends. You know, it was the thing to do. My friends—they all went crazy. They bought albums, snow globes, carnation arrangements in the shape of Teddy Bears to lay near the eternal flame. Not me. I was sensible.

It was my friend Nina who started all this. I wanted an angel for the top of my tree, and I didn't like anything I saw in the stores. So Nina—who's a potter—as a joke—she made me the King of Kings. A ceramic Elvis, with wings.

I didn't buy any of these ornaments. Not the 12 Hound dogs howling; or the 11 teddies bears twisting; 10 blue Hawaii leis; 9 pink Cadillacs; 8 fat Elvi; 7 in black leather; 6 wearing gold suits; 5 blue suede shoes (which was really Carl Perkins' hit); 4 Colonel Parkers; 3 Kid Creoles; 2 Pricilla Presleys; and 1 heartbreak hotel.

I have to admit, I love the tree skirt. It's based on the capes from the Fat Elvis period. And these bows are made out of scarves that Elvis threw to his audience. The spots are Elvis' personal sweat stains. Gross, but expensive.

It's a big thing now. Everybody buys me Elvis ornaments. I draw the line at magnets, tea towels, china, spoons, paintings, basically anything that doesn't fit neatly on a fir branch.

I couldn't live with this schlock year-round, but Christmas only comes once a year.

My mother thinks I'm desecrating the tradition of the Christmas tree. But, I mean it's not like anyone I know worships tinsel or popcorn or bells. Elvis' dominating presence on my tree is not an affront to God.

Though my Elvis Nativity might be. My last relationship made it for me. See, it's the shack in Tupelo, Mississippi, where he was born. And here's baby Elvis lying in an old truck tire. Mama and Daddy gaze upon him in wonder, and the Angel of the Lord is Sam Phillips of Sun Records. Yeah, it is sacrilegious.

Last year, I got a Hallmark Keepsake Ornament of the Wicked Witch from the *Wizard of Oz*. I had to take her off the tree. She didn't fit in. I suppose I could get rid of all the Elvis stuff. Start over again with some tinsel and red ribbon. But the truth is, I've come to like my tree.

Not because I'm being postmodern. I'm not wonderfully camp. Or hysterically retro. I'm not being witty.

I think that Elvis embodies the Christmas message. It wouldn't surprise me if Elvis eventually co-opts Christianity. Think about it. Elvis and Christ were only children born in humble circumstances. Both thought their mothers were virgins. Devoted followers sighted them after their deaths. Miracles have been attributed to both. Elvis' fans have petitioned the Pope to make him a saint, even though Elvis is not Catholic. Jesus' fans founded Christianity, though he was not a Christian.

And they had very similar goals. All Christ wanted us to do was love one another. Elvis wanted everybody to dance. They made people happy. Attracted frenzied mobs. Jew, Roman, Tax Collector, Samaritans, Black, White, you name it. Many diverse cultures were unified in their love of these men.

Elvis sang for everyone. But he wasn't very happy. He suffered terribly before he died. Maybe it was the drugs, the lost youth. Or maybe he had simply lost his way. That's something I can identify with.

We try so hard to get something out of life. Most of us don't get anything. Some of us achieve our wildest dreams. Then what? Elvis bought Graceland for his mother and she died soon after. There's nothing sadder than an empty house.

I think Elvis lost his soul somewhere in that mansion. I've been back to Graceland twice now, looking for the spirit that was the man. It's not in the Jungle room, or on the giant white couch. It's certainly not in the display of costumes that he wore. Last summer I went to Vegas. They play *Viva Las Vegas* a lot, but aside from that, there wasn't any Elvis. Perhaps because they're such commercial venues. One shouldn't have to pay to go to church.

My tree is free. This is the time of year for healing the soul. I sit here, alone, watching the lights late at night. I look at my Elvis Nativity, and as my gaze drifts from the base to the very top of the tree where my winged Elvis wafts, I reflect on the past year. I plan for the coming one. And I pray for Elvis. I know he's dead. I hope his soul is healing. That he is with his beloved mother. That he is free from pain. God, I hope he's happy. He deserves his happiness.

Can I get you a drink?

Teddy '77

ANDRÉA J. ONSTAD

August, the present. "Jesse's Gas," a service station in Batesville, Mississippi, junction of U.S. 6 and 51. A billboard above the gas station—an outline of a near-naked female, part human, part angel, part car, with automobile headlights for breasts that blink on and off and the words, "Angel's Back Room. Let an Angel Fix Your Car." Angel, a middle-aged female mechanic, wears greasy coveralls.

ANGEL (*To audience*): Howdy, folks. Want a fill-up? Gotta wait for Jess to come out of the crapper. He does all the gassin', oilin', window washin', and tire fillin' around here. Want an oil change, engine overhaul, tranny rebuilt, you got the right gal. What's that? Oh, you want a fill-up AND directions. Well, I can give you them directions but you all gotta wait for Jess for the fill-up and just to warn you, it might be a while. He took the August issue of *Popular Mechanics* in with him. That boy sure tries to learn how to fix cars but he just don't never catch on. But if you're runnin' on empty, you're best off waitin' 'cause there ain't no tellin' how far you gotta go up the road to find the next service station that ain't closed down.

Let me guess, I bet you all are goin' to Memphis, right? All you do is just get on 55 there, that's the Interstate, oh about a mile east of here, head north and Memphis is about, oh, 50 miles or so up the road. You'll run right into it.

Oh, you know HOW to get to Memphis, you want to know what exit to take IN Memphis to get to Graceland. Well, you know, I ain't never been there but I know the address by heart, 3764 Elvis Presley Boulevard, 'cause I almost got there once, right in this here car right here.

Hey, this ain't no piece of junk. This here is my blue '68 Chevy Camaro convertible. Dual exhaust. V-8. Four-on-the-floor. Supersport. Got everything. You name it. Built her up myself. Check this out. Keep your eyes on her headlights—yes, they still work—kept her battery up, too. Okay, keep watchin' . . . keep watchin' . . . Did you see that? Did you see her covers open up and go blink-blink? Yep, like my sign. I'll do it again. See? Blink-blink. Just like real eyelids, huh? Been thinkin' I should fix her up again, get her on the road, put falsies on her so everybody'll know when Nadia hits the streets. No, not them kind of falsies. My, ain't you all got dirty little minds.

Nadia, that's right. I named her Nadia for that gymnast back in the '70s. Remember her? Yeah, Comaneci. 'Cause my blue wonder car here performed like an Olympic champ. Back in August '77, it was Tuesday, the 16th, me and her, we was gettin' ready to shoot up U.S. 55 and head for heaven. Me and her, we was gonna leave Jackson and all its Mississippi pines and billboards behind forever. Me and her, we was gonna have a new life, just like the real Nadia, with fame and fortune, 'cause we was goin' to Graceland, goin' to see The King. Me and him, we was simpatico. Yeah. 'Cause we was both in the entertainment industry.

Just outside of Jackson I pulled into this Gulf station to get some gas, just like you folks is doin' now, and this tall, handsome young man comes over, leans down and says, "Can I help you, ma'am?"

My heart was just a poundin' 'cause this young man was the spittin' image of Elvis Presley, hair all pompadoured, that little sexy lift of the lip, the whole shebang. Actually I thought he might be one of them Elvis impersonators 'cause Mississippi was stampin' them out like cookies back then. So anyways, I said, "You sure can. You can fill 'er up." So I was watchin' him fillin' up my tank and washin' the windows and I said, "You like my car? '68 Supersport. V-8. Four-on-the-floor. Got everything"—I told him all that stuff.

And he blushed and said, "Sure do, ma'am."

So I told him to stand in front of the headlights and I turned on Nadia's lights, just like I did for you all, and he blushed and said, "She sure is something."

And then I said, "You know, you could do something else for me," and I paused just to watch him blush again, then I said, "You could give me some directions, too. I'm goin' to Graceland."

And his eyes lit all up and sparkled and he said, "Well, I ain't never been there but I sure know the address, it's 3764 Elvis Presley Boulevard."

So I kinda teased him then some more, you know, I WAS flirtin' 'cause he was so darn cute, and I says, "Yeah, me and Elvis, we're simpatico 'cause we're both in the entertainment industry." He was checkin' the oil, the hood was raised up, and I says, "I bet you wanna know my expertise" and I kinda wiggled my shoulders just a little, just enough to loosen my coat. I had one of them trenchcoats on, the kind flashers wear, even though it was dog days and hotter than you know what, but I was wearin' this coat, see, 'cause all I had on underneath was this little peekaboo teddy, so I just kinda wiggled my shoulders just a little bit so he'd catch a little of the lace when he'd come by my window and there he comes, holdin' that dipstick in two hands like he was showin' me a newborn, and I says, "Don't you wanna know?" and he's noddin' and his Adam's apple's bobbin' just like Eve had just shoved it down his throat so I let my coat drop off one shoulder and I says, "I'll tell you if you ride along" and I let the coat drop off of the other shoulder and says, "I could use the company" and I let the coat slip down my arms and says, "Plus you could keep me awake when the NoDoze wears off" and I let it slide all the way to my waist and says, "Maybe I'll even let you take the wheel a little bit" and then I slide my arms out of the coat sleeves and lean over to the window towards him, just enough so he can get a full view beyond the lace and I says, "I really need someone who can remember the address."

That sure lit a fire under that slow-movin' Mississippi boy! He was tryin' to put the dipstick back in and missin', slammin' the hood and it wasn't catchin', ringin' up the sale and droppin' coins and I tell him, "Keep the change," so he grabs a couple Kit-Kats off the candy rack and jumps in next to me just as his manager comes out of the crapper, combin' his hair.

"Hey, boy!" he yells, "Where do you think you're goin'?"

"I rang it all up, sir," my boy yells back, and I squeal off.

His Gulf Oil cap flew off his head, spun in the air a few times, and landed right smack in the station's doorway like that was all was left of him.

And then, right there sittin' next to me is Elvis' spittin' image.

"Your shirt says 'Jesse Gulf Oil.' That your name?"

"Yes, ma'am," he says.

"Okay. So, Mr. Oil, do you go by your first name, 'Jesse', or your middle name, 'Gulf', or do you prefer 'Mr. Oil'?"

"Ma'am," he says, "I don't mean no disrespect, but my middle name ain't 'Gulf' and I ain't no 'Oil.' You can call me 'Jesse.'"

"Okay. Jesse what?"

"Jesse Garon, ma'am."

"Jesse Garon! That's Elvis Presley's twin brother's name. You're pullin' my leg," I says.

"No, ma'am, I ain't pullin' your leg."

And I feel his eyes burnin' a hole through my right thigh, right where the trench coat is kinda fallin' away, and I says, "No, but you're burnin' a hole through my right one." And I peak over and see him blushin'. "You sure you ain't Elvis Presley's twin?"

"No, ma'am," he says.

"Well, you sure look like a Presley," I says, "you even got that little lift-of-the-lip half-grin when you smile, which I hope I'll see a little more of."

"Yes, ma'am," he says.

I was joshin' him. I knew he was too young, but I liked seein' him blush. It went all the way up into the roots of his hair, which was that kind you can't tell if it's light brown or blonde, the kind you can't buy out of a bottle, the kind Elvis really had.

"Guess you're too young anyways," I says.

"Yes, ma'am."

"You could be his son."

"Yes, ma'am."

"Your mom, did she like Elvis?"

"Yes, ma'am."

"Are you his son?"

"No, ma'am. At least, I don't think so, ma'am."

"You don't talk much, do you?"

"No, ma'am."

"That's okay. I been known to do the talkin' for a whole room of people, guess I can do it for you, too."

Then I says to him, "The first chance we get, we're gonna get rid of that borin' shirt you got there with your name tag on it like some kind of dorky conventiongoer and get you one made outta gold lamé. Would you like that?" And before he can spit it out, I says, "Yes, ma'am! See?" I says, "I can read your mind!" And he blushes all the way to the ends of his pompadour. The back of his neck is as red as a Coke can.

Boy, she sure is a hot one today. Say, folks, you all wouldn't want a Coke or something, would you? We got plenty of Coke. Jess's takin' so long and I know better than to bother him when he's in there with a new *Popular Mechanics*. I got a cold case in the cooler. I can just bring it out and you all can just help yourselves.

So, anyways, I says to Jess, "You like these seats? Color of cream cheese. Like me. That's what my ex-as-of-today says. Said me and him couldn't make it 'cause of my thing for Elvis. Said Elvis was nothin' but a thief, said he stole all his ideas for music and clothes and stuff from his people. I couldn't explain. I mean, how can you explain Elvis? What was there to say except 'toodle-oo.' So I said, 'Toodle-oo.'"

"These seats are cozy, huh? You can really get your tush all snuggled in. Yeah, I love this tuck and roll. Got it in Nogales. Drove 90 miles per, night and day, 'til I got there. Nogales-Nogales. Went right across the border to the first reupholster shop and said, 'Do it, boys, por favor.' Yeah. Hecho in Mexico. Sat there the whole time makin' sure they wouldn't plant nothin' in the seats. I drank so much Fanta that day waitin' I was afraid I'd turn the seats orange on the way back. Had the top done, too, by a sailmaker. See? I push this button, like this, and chica chica boom! Cucaracha! We got a main mast! But me, I like speedboats. I say take down the sails, turn on the motor, and fly over that water. Let the spray hit your face like a facial, let the breeze mess up your hair so no beauty parlor can ever get the tangles out, and let the sun beat down and turn that cream cheese into chocolate. That's what I say. It's like bein' in a little piece of heaven, ain't it. Nadia's a little chunk of blue sky—'cept I've been thinkin' of paintin' her Elvis Cadillac-Pink—and these white seats here are the clouds, and me, I'm the angel. You like angels, Jesse?"

"Yes, ma'am," he says.

"Well, that's what they call me at the club. 'Oh Angel, bring me a beer, Angel.' 'Keep the change, Angel. That's right. All of it.' 'How about a table dance, Angel?' 'Hey, Angel, when is it your turn to get up there and shake?' 'Oh you big old teddy bears,' I tell 'em. They all liked that teddy bear-kootchy-koo stuff so much I rounded up all the stuffed teddy bears my exes won for me—yeah, that's them in the back there—and I brought them all into the club along with my Elvis 'Teddy Bear' tape—'Oh why don't you let me be/Your teddy bear'—you know, that one—and I piled them all up on stage and I got up there in my baby dolls and pigtails, yawnin' and everything, and then I just started wigglin' around. They loved it. Bet you'd love it, too, wouldn't you, Jesse?"

And what do you think he said to that, folks? That's right! Say it with me, you all. "Yes, ma'am!"

So, yeah, I was in the entertainment industry and my expertise was dancin'. Go-go. To all The King's songs, but especially "Teddy Bear"—"I don't wanna be your lion/I don't wanna be your tiger"—I had moves to that song. When it was time for my pillow dance, I'd wear that little tiny teddy peekaboo and G-string I had on that day and I'd get down on my great big old teddy bear and just groove. Bet you all can't believe it, way I look now. Don't answer that, folks.

So anyways, when I told Jess I was a go-go dancer, his eyes almost fell out of his head. He actually turned around in his seat and said something to me without my havin' to pry it out of him. He said, "Oh, ma'am, I ain't never met a real go-go dancer."

I thought that young boy was gonna have a premature heart attack.

Didn't know I was gonna say, "heart attack," did you folks?

So I says to him, "Tell you what. I'm gonna give you a go-go lesson right here, right now. Let me put this tape in first. Made this here tape myself. Both sides. All 'Teddy Bear.' See? Side One: 'Teddy Bear,' 'Teddy Bear,' 'Teddy Bear,' 'Teddy Bear,' 'Teddy Bear,' 'Teddy Bear,' 'Teddy Bear,' and 'Teddy Bear, continued.' Side Two: 'Teddy Bear, continued'—I hate to lose even one note of it I love it so much—'Teddy Bear,' 'Teddy Bear,' 'Teddy Bear,' 'Teddy Bear,' 'Teddy Bear,' 'Teddy Bear,' and at the very end I say, 'I love you, Elvis.'"

"Okay, we're ready." I says, "And we're all cued up to . . ."

"'Teddy Bear,' ma'am!" he says.

"Good. You're payin' attention," I says. "Okay, you feel that opening?"

"Yes, ma'am," he says.

"I mean, you got to feel the music," I tell him, "not just hear it, and after you feel the music you've got to feel his voice. I move to his voice. Hear that tremolo he does right there?—'Ohhoholet me be'—that 'Ohhoho' really gets me. I feel it and move to it, see?"

"Yes, ma'am," he says.

"It don't matter how you move, just move how you feel. Still not gettin' it?"

"No, ma'am," he says.

"Okay," I says. "Secret. The trick is to dance under the music, you know, not with the music, not on the beat, but just kind of under it, see? Slooooooooooooow. Try it—it's hard, ain't it?"

"Yes, ma'am."

"You still don't feel it?"

"No, ma'am."

"Really?"

"Yes, ma'am."

"Well," I tell him, "I guess that's what makes me an artist. They call me that sometimes, you know. 'Angel, you're a real artist up there,' they say. And I say, 'Well, then buy me a drink' and I snap my fingers and Carol comes over and I say, 'Carol, bring me the usual, this little teddy bear here is buyin'' and Carol says, 'And what a cute little teddy bear,' and he just grins from ear to ear. And then she goes up to Jay, he's the bartender, and she tells him, 'Angel's got a sleeper. Fix her the usual' and Jay'll grumble, 'Oh you girls and your B-drinks' and then he'll start to pour a glass of tonic and in midstream he'll say, 'Heck, I'll give her a double. Tell that sleeper he's gettin' a two-for-one special. We'll make him stay all day.' And then old Jay'll stick in a lime—I like lime, not lemon—and then, if I squeeze the teddy just a little and chuck him under his chin and call him 'my teddy bear' before Carol gets back, he'll tip her a five, and when she's gone he'll slip a twenty under the table for me, aimin' it right between my legs but I can usually grab it before he scores, and if Roxanne just happens to be squattin' on top of his nose up there at the end of the runway, she gets a fin, too. And guess where? Right in her cleavage! Shocked you, didn't I?"

79

Oh, I had that boy blushin'.

Yeah, I was gonna dance for The King. I had it all planned out. I was gonna go up to them gates at Graceland and say, "I gotta see Elvis 'cause I'm an angel—I'm The Angel—and I'm here to dance for The King." And they woulda called him up on the intercom and he woulda answered, "Send that little darlin' right on up." And I woulda drove on through them gates and parked right in front and he woulda been there himself, waitin' just for me, and I was gonna try not to look too shocked 'cause, after all, he weighed about two fifty back then and I wasn't gonna tell him how he looked like he'd gone to pot, I was gonna save that for pillow talk later. And on the way up to his room I was gonna wave to the Memphis Mafia sittin' there in his livin' room, I was gonna say, "Howdy boys," like I'd known them all my life, and I was gonna follow Elvis up them stairs right into his bedroom where I woulda seen that famous nine-foot-square double-king-sized bed and the mirrors and them huge picture windows all blacked out like a Vegas show room. And I was gonna say, "Elvis, this here is nice, but I just want you to sing 'Teddy Bear' for me," and right there in his bedroom I'dda picked up one of his guitars layin' there and handed it to him and then I'dda stood in front of the blacked-out windows with the big drapes hangin' all around like a stage and I'dda shucked off my coat 'cause I'dda had on that peekaboo teddy I was wearin' and I'dda had some of them teddy bears I always carried in the back seat right in my hand and I'dda set 'em up like I did at the club. And he woulda been strummin' a few chords and then he woulda said, "Little darlin' I wanna show you something first. Come on down to my office." And he woulda been strummin' as I'dda been followin' him down the steps and then he woulda opened a door and there'd be that room I'd read about in the movie magazines, all filled with teddy bears, so many teddy bears you'd never believe there could be that many teddy bears in the world and I'dda said, "Oh, Elvis, I've never seen so many teddy bears." And he woulda said, "Little darlin', jump right up on that desk there and we'll do a little number together." And right there in front of the wall where all his gold records were hangin' would be his desk and on it the sign that said, "Elvis, The Boss," just like it showed in the pictures, and I'dda kicked off my blue suede spikes and jumped right up there and he woulda started playin', for real now, not just strummin' and hummin', and I'dda wiggled my bare toes, tickled the "B" in "Boss" and felt his voice goin' right through me as I moooooooved. I'dda closed my eyes and got to soarin' with him on the notes like I was right there with him in front of thousands.

Oh I wouldda loved it.

So I was tellin' Jess my whole dream when all of a sudden I see this sign, "Tupelo—Next Exit—Highway 6 East— 10 Miles," and I says, "Hey, will you look at that! Let's go to Tupelo, pay our respects to Elvis' birthplace and THEN go to Graceland. Know that address?"

"306 Elvis Presley Boulevard, used to be Old Saltillo road, ma'am," he says.

"Boy, you ARE good to have around, ain't you?"

"Yes, ma'am," he says.

"Well, let's step on it then."

And what do you know, the dang truck that's been tailin' us the last half hour comes right up alongside of us and both them truckers in there are lookin' down at us and gawkin' and pointin' and makin' obscene gestures—honestly, grown men act like little kids sometimes—so I holler up at them, "Hey boys, what you lookin' at? Ain't you never seen a gal drivin' a convertible before?" and I kick off my spike heel so I can feel that metal and really concentrate holdin' Nadia steady, and I press my toe down hard and I says, "Come on, Nadia. Let's go! We're in the Olympics now! So long, boys!" And we tore up that highway. That big old Peterbilt was nothin' but a speck in the rearview mirror in a matter of seconds.

"You know, Jesse," I says after I ease off a bit, "my big dream is to do a real show with El. I mean, since we're both entertainers, we ought to be able to do a show together, right?"

"Yes, ma'am," he says.

"See, I got this idea for an act, where I dress up in an angel teddy with wings and a halo and stuff and I come floatin' in on a cloud and an Elvis impersonator just below me is singin' 'Teddy Bear' live, not canned, and I sit there and wiggle around on this big ball of cotton and tickle his toupee with my toes. I wanted Ron, he's the club manager, to get me flyin' equipment so I could do it. I said I'd hire the imperson- ator myself. Heck, if I woulda known you just yesterday I'dda asked you. You woulda done it, wouldn't you?"

"Yes, ma'am," he says.

"But Ron wouldn't go for it. Said if he wouldn't do it for the real big shows he sure as heck wouldn't do it for me. But, he said, if I got some silicon injections he might reconsider, and then he put his hands on me and twisted what little I *do* have like radio dials. Made me so mad I slapped 'em off and said, 'Hell'—yeah, I said 'hell,' I don't like to swear but I had to let him know I meant business—so I said, 'Hell, I know where I can go to get some real production values. I'm goin' to The King himself. Me and him, we'll do it. Screw you and your show,' and I walked off. Just like that. But hey, it's okay. Me and El. We're gonna tour. I just know it. But, Jesse, tell me the truth now. Do you think I need silicon injections?"

And Jess looks over at me and I kind of stick them out there so he can get a better assessment and he says, "No, ma'am, you sure don't."

And then I see "Tupelo This Exit," and we're comin' right up on it, just barely takin' the curve, when all of a sud- den there's this BOOM! and Nadia's rockin' and rollin' like we're on high seas with a hurricane comin' in and I'm white-knucklin' the wheel so tight I'm pressin' prints into the leather at the same time I'm takin' my foot off the gas and screamin', "Blowout! Front tire blowout!" and Jess's reachin' over grabbin' at the wheel and I'm screamin' at him, "I got it! I got it! Get your hands off! You'll turn us over!" and I start to ease down on the brake, my heart's goin' thumpathumpathumpa and then I realize my heart, Jess' heart and the wheel are all goin' thunkathunkathunka thunka thunka thunka all at the same time as I roll her to a stop. And wouldn't you know, here comes that same darn Peterbilt and sure enough, it's slowin' down, and I says to Jess, "I ain't flaggin' down no trucker and I ain't flaggin' down no highway patrol. I'll fix her myself. Nobody touches this car, and I mean nobody. Come on. Out. I ain't jackin' her up with your hinder in it."

And then, there they come, the rubberneckers. And it ain't just the Peterbilt that stops, it's a whole truck lot of 'em, Freightliners, Kenworths, Macks, the whole works. And they're all gettin' out of their trucks, just as nosey as dumb old clucks in a farmyard—gotta know everything. And I'm openin' the trunk and gettin' the jack and crawlin' around settin' her up and all the time I'm answerin' their questions:

"No boys, I don't need no help, I know what I'm doin'."

"No."

"No, thanks."

"No! Thank! You!"

"No, you can't have my phone number."

"Ain't your business what I got on under this here coat."

"No, I won't show you. You want a show, you gotta pay. Now get out of here."

"Get lost!"

"I mean it! Beat it!"

And I get her all set up and I'm just standin' there, lookin' at her, cryin' a little, "Oh Nadia, how could you do this to me. Just look at your tire!" And Jess's just standin' over there on the shoulder, kickin' stones, I think 'cause he ain't helpin' none and all them men see that, so I holler at him, "Hey, why don't you hand me that wrench there in the trunk, then turn on the radio, find some good tire changin' music, turn it up real loud."

And Jess comes back with a little old crescent wrench from my toolbox and I hate to embarrass him but I say, kinda gentle-like, "No, not that wrench, dummy, the tire wrench," and while he's back there fiddlin' in the trunk again, I tell him, "Don't worry, Jesse. We're still gonna get to Graceland. I promise. We're gonna see them music notes on the gate, just like the Gate of Heaven. And El's gonna be there strummin' on a harp, singin' his heart out on some gospel song or other. He likes gospel, you know. He sings it real good, too. Church music. You know," I says, "when I get done dancin', when I don't look good nomore, I'm gonna open me up a garage, that's what I'm savin' my money for, that's what I really want to talk to El about, the future, me and him, he likes his motorcycles and me, I like my cars. We're gonna be tight."

And then my patience runs out and I yell, "Forget the wrench! I'll get the wrench! Just turn on that radio! I need some lug nut-twistin', car-jackin' music to work by. We're darn close to Memphis, something's gotta come in, even with my coat hanger aerial, and that something better be The King." And I start singin' as I'm messin' around in the trunk, gettin' the tire wrench, goin' back over to the tire and loosenin' the nuts—"That's all right, mama/That's all right by me."

"Hey, ma'am," Jess yells out a little crabby-like, "I can't hear nothin' with you singin' like that."

"All right, all right, singin' ain't my specialty no ways."

And then the last lug nut comes off and I'm still only hearin' static so I holler, "Hey, forget the station for a minute and roll that spare on over here." And my back's kinda crimpin' so I stand up straight and kinda glance over to where all them trucks I been ignorin' are and see the last one pullin' out just as Jess says, "Ma'am, the spare's flat."

"What do you mean, the spare's flat?" I yell at him like it's his fault. "Can't be. I put air in that thing myself. Let me see."

And he bounces it, presses down on it and sure enough, it's as flat as a pancake.

"Oh man," I say. "Oh man, oh man, oh man."

And he lets it flop down in the dust.

So I walk over to the car, the driver's side, reach in and switch the radio over to AM, the poor dumb boy had it on FM and that don't come in hardly ever with my rigged aerial, and sure enough, I'm gettin' a signal, loud and clear, but what I'm hearin' next is something I really can't believe, even more than I couldn't believe my spare was flat. This DJ is sayin', "In our tribute to Elvis, we're gonna play all of his hits, and there were a lot of hits, folks, a lot of hits. And for those of you listeners out there just tuning in, The King is dead."

I musta passed out then 'cause the next thing I know is I'm lookin' up towards the highway from my ant's eye view down there on the ground and I see Jess standin' out there with his thumb out.

"Jesse," I yell out to him as I crawl over to the spare layin' there in the dirt. "Where you goin'?" And I pull myself up onto the spare and I'm sittin' there with my head between my knees, cryin' and beggin' like a child, "Jesse, please don't go. Come over here and sit by me for just one minute. Please."

And he comes over but that moon-eyed look is gone from his eyes and he's lookin' down at me, kinda cold-like. And I says, "Please. Sit by me."

And he sits but he keeps as much distance from me as he can in such close quarters, makin' sure we don't touch at all. And I say, "Jess, I got me another idea. I got me some money saved, let's me and you open a garage, right here, right in this very spot. You'll pump the gas and I'll run the back room. We'll have a big old sign that says, 'Jesse's Gas' and another one that says 'Angel's Back Room and Tire Service,' what do you say?"

"Yes, ma'am!" he shouts and jumps up, all excited now.

"You don't have to 'ma'am' me no more, Jess."

"Yes, ma'am!" he shouts again.

"Just remember, I don't want you touchin' the cars. Stick to the gas. Now turn off that dang radio, I don't wanna hear no more about it."

"Yes, ma'am!"

And that was the last "ma'am!" I ever heard out of him, folks. The sign changed a little over the years and, I guess, so did me and Jess, but hey, I didn't have no more exes, 'cause he ain't never left me and I ain't never left him. Just as long as we both just stick to our specialties, we get along just fine.

Oh listen. I think Jess's on his way. I can hear him flushin'.

Hey, what did you do, read the whole dang magazine? Don't do you no good no ways.

Okay, folks. He'll be here in a minute. I gotta get back in the garage. Clean up a little. Pick up my tools. But, hey, you all have a nice trip, you hear? And send me a postcard from Graceland. Folks just like you travellin' from all over stop in here all the time on their way to Graceland and I tell them all the same, "Send me a postcard when you get there." I got hundreds of 'em plastered all over my back room like some mechanics got girlie calendars. I got me so many postcards of Graceland, I know the place inside and out, don't never need to go there now.

Hey Jess, get your butt on over here. These folks been waitin' almost an hour.

Hey, good talkin' to you all and listen, stop in again sometime, you hear? And don't you forget "Angel's Back Room." You need a tune-up, oil change, engine overhaul, tranny rebuilt? You just let an angel fix your car. You need gas? You gotta wait for Jess. We're here, right on the outskirts of heaven.

Resignation

MURRAY HORWITZ

Scene: an office. A man sits at desk, facing audience. There is a telephone on his desk.

MAN: What?!? Well, you can quit if you wanna. But I'mma tell you what: you walk out that door, boy, don't bother t'come on back. You gonna be wantin' a dollar twenty-five a hour a couple weeks from now, and I'mma tell you what—I'm not goin' give it to you. Jus' where you think you are, boy? This is Memphis, Tennessee!

I know what you been doin'. Been aroun' town singin' that ol' Shake Rag music. Boy, don't nobody wanna hear that stuff. An' sure as hell don' wanna hear it up in Nashville. Them folks up there. Who you think you are, some Frankie Laine? You ain't even no whatsisname—that boy that died?— Hank? Hank somethin'? Boy, you don't play no hillbilly music. (*Pause*) You know, I thought you had a future here. I really did. Boy like you. Dependable. I had my eye on you. I did. 'Cause I can see it in a young man. An' I'm not wrong about people. You got ideas, I can see that. But you . . . Boy, take my advice. Don't—(*Sighs*) Nashville. "The Grand Ol' Opry." Boy . . .

Well. I don't know anymore. This here game done passed me by somewheres. A dollar twenty-five a hour. That's more than minimum wage! For a young punk like you. Shit. When I was your age . . .

Well, go on. Get out o' here. But I'mma tell you what. You take my advice, you'll get back in that truck an' realize you got a good thing here. (*Phone rings*) But, like I said, you

x

87

walk out now, don't bother comin' back. (*Phone rings. Man picks it up*) You hear me, boy? (*Into phone*) Crown 'lectric.

Blackout

Land for Elvis

SHARON HOUCK ROSS

Laneece enters hesitantly and looks around.

LANEECE: Oh my. It looks so different now . . . what you've done in here in Mother's house. Excuse me, *your* house now, yours for five years, now. My goodness—all this black leather, the sofa, and the red velvet drapes. It looks just like Grace-land. Even the piano.

I wonder what Mother would say? You know how she felt about Tom Jones. I kept tellin her, "Mama, Tom Jones is a teensie weensie little fella. The TV makes him look big like Elvis, but in real life? He wouldn't even reach the tip of your chin." She never did believe me.

She should've gone with us to see Elvis live in Shreveport. She would've seen the difference then. He was already fat but it didn't matter one bit. "Love Me Tender." "Teddy Bear." And best of all, "I Taught Her How." Sister had to take a Val-ium. You fainted out loud. I brought along a brown paper bag in case I hyperventilated. I did, but I never let go of my binoculars the whole time.

You still have his driver's license and Cadillac plates? Me too. That white scarf with a drop of real sweat on it? Me too. How about that hound dog that sings "Are You Lonesome Tonight"—does yours still work? Oh good. Mine started stickin'.

She pauses, smiles tightly. She tries to take a deep breath, but has difficulty.

Oh, look here at your Elvis ring collection. Aren't they displayed so nice in that fancy case. I still have just my one. I swear to God, it's the best birthday present Jug ever gave me. He slid it on my other ring finger and it fit like I was born to it. Oh, here can you see it? You remember it, don't you? The picture is a little faded from doin' the dishes, I guess, but he's still there. Oh no. I can't let you hold it. I never take it off. I haven't taken it off since that day I let you wear it at the Horseshoe Casino.

Oh Lord, that quarter machine was eatin' your tokens like Chicken McNuggets. You were having one long streak of evil luck. And then I let you wear Elvis. Are you rememberin' any of this? At first it didn't do you any good and you got p.o.'ed and whopped that machine upside its head. I looked up in time to see Elvis leave my ring, his picture I mean, and roll right under the seat of a machine three stools down. Well that was your lucky machine wasn't it? How much did you end up winnin' that day? Something over $800? I never saw so many quarters in one place in all my life.

You know, I was in old man Lester's store the other day, and he offered me $1,000 for this ring. I said I wouldn't sell it for a million. And I meant it. Jug said that was the day two fools met. Cause he'd only paid $19.95 for it in Memphis and the picture wasn't even glued on good.

She's having trouble breathing. She takes out a small paper bag from her purse and breathes into it a couple of times.

I'm sorry. I guess it's being back in this house for the first time in five years. I guess maybe I was hopin' to find something of Mother left in here, you know.

You dream about her? I do. All the time. We're sittin' out there on the front porch—you, me, Sister, and Mama—drinkin' sun tea and laughin' and talkin', just about silly everyday things, you know, like we used to. She's shellin' purple hull peas.

It took me three years to get a handle on my grief after she died. I couldn't even pass this house without chokin'.

How do you think it made Sister and me feel, you takin' a peace bond out against us? Forbiddin' us to enter our own mother's house.

I never will forgive you for what you did after she died. I've tried. I've prayed on it. But I can't. Mama always said she was leavin' everything equal to all of us. She even made us pick out the pieces of land we wanted. And when the will was read at the funeral home? It was just like she said it would be. Then three days later, here you come up with another one. Leavin' everything to you. Mother would never, never do such a thing.

No, don't you open your mouth. Don't you even look at me with the idea of "signature" in your eye. Even I could forge Mother's signature. And that's what you did. I know it and you know it. But you know who doesn't? Sister. And she's still hurtin'. She'll go to her grave wonderin' why Mama died mad at her.

That day she came over here to buy back her own land from you—you were cleanin' out the closet in the kitchen— and you remember what you said to her? You said, "No. I want to keep it in the *family*." You said that to your own sister. She started cryin' and just turned around and walked home. If I was her, I woulda pushed your skinny butt into that closet, slammed the door and moved the refrigerator in front of it.

She crumples up the paper bag and stuffs it back into her purse.

And for your information, I went to Dr. Jacobs in Marshall. I made an appointment, special, and I asked him point-blank what killed Mama. He said it was just that her heart gave out. She was old and her heart was tired. It wasn't anybody's fault. Not Sister's. Not mine. I can't believe you could blame us like that. Mama worried more about you alone than she ever did about Sister and me combined. We didn't get ourselves pregnant and drop out of school, did we? No ma'am.

We didn't marry a man who had more money than he had brain cells. And we raised our kids on our own. We didn't drop them off here every summer for Mama to take care of.

And let me tell you something else. If Mama could see what you've done to her house, she'd up and die all over again. You don't even live here. You just lock it up like some museum and come visit when you're feelin' lonely for Elvis. Well, Elvis never treated his family like you've treated yours. And if Mama knew what you were doin', she'd take a switch to your legs.

I came over here for a reason today. I want that land for Sister. She's alone, now that Terrance has passed. She needs to move her trailer to some place permanent. Don't give me that look. I know you don't need the money. It's not money I'm offerin'. It's this.

She holds up her hand with the Elvis ring on it.

That's right. You need this, don't you? Yes, I know you do. And not just for your Elvis collection, either. Everybody in Uncertain knows you're having another streak of evil luck with Mason. He may have a lot of money, but that don't make him less of a tomcat, does it? And I hear tell how he's serious about this latest little gal from Longview. Yeah, it's gettin' harder and harder to hold onto that rich tomcat, now that you're pushin' forty, isn't it?

Well, here's how it works. You pick up that phone and you call your Big Sister and you apologize. You tell her how you've had a change of heart and you are hereby deeding her land back to her.

You do that and I'll give you this ring. Not a word leaves this house. Land for Elvis. Deal?

She waits, wiggling her Elvis ring finger. Then she smiles and takes it off.

Deal.

The Draw

JAMES R. MILLER

Jesse, the stillborn twin brother of Elvis Aron Presley, was delivered first, and the doctor was uncertain whether the second child would be alive either. But Elvis was delivered some thirty minutes later, alive and healthy. Jesse was buried the next day in an unmarked grave in the Priceville Cemetery near East Tupelo, Mississippi.

JESSE: If only I could hear your whispers now. Those soft Southern syllables that my throat would never pronounce, falling from the corner of your trademark upturned lips, when the door pushed back on a sea of faces and you finally turned the latch for the night. You and I, brother, we were quite a team. Your flesh and blood so similar to mine as it once was . . . as it could've been.

You had secret crooked smiles for shadows you were never sure existed. But I was always present. You just looked in all the wrong places.

Oh, I could've hated you. I can see how you believed that. But not for the fame and fortune, not even for the women. Just for that one woman, our mother, whose soft skin absorbed your newborn warmth, while the universe collected the fumes from my own cooling body. Yeah, I could've hated you for that. Somehow it's always seemed like the only bad part of the deal.

But we both know, there would have been no Elvis, had there been a Jesse. We were told that before we drew. Some other handsome kid from some other no-name Southern town would've made it . . . the time was just ripe. Together we would have been too busy for thoughts of singing or romance. You would have never received that guitar for your eleventh birthday, we would've had boxing gloves or baseball mitts or something. And that high school hairstyle of yours, I'd have kicked your butt my damned self, and no Red West would've been there to stop me.

Oh, but the truth is, brother, when the time came for you to enter the world, you begged to stay behind.

Even in the womb, you had already seen too much.

Somehow, you managed to glance through my drying, lifeless eyes, transformed as they were, images unutterable flashing before them.

And in that moment, you caught on to the rhythm of another plane. You discovered the truth about sound, about vibration evoking each emotion, love and lust, anger, hate, rage and beauty, so much beauty, that it filled you within, exploding each time you took the stage. You were our Prometheus, sharing your music with mankind. And although this was powerful, life-giving information, it was too much for one single man to harbor.

And so you rushed through life, living months in each day, and eternities in drugged-out nights. You thought the momentum would bring you back to me quicker, and together again, we would conquer this obstacle.

But the secret is, Elvis, that there is no back, and brother, an even bigger secret is, there is no me.

My lives number two. Once fleeting and flesh, sprawled like a naked costume, bloody in the mess of the birth waste on the floor of your future home.

And then, for the rest of your life, inside the painted walls of your sheltered mind. I existed within you all along. And only within you. Your whispers made me real, your need for someone just to understand. Somehow you thought that your birth had robbed me of life, but brother, it was you who rebirthed me.

You raised me up alongside you. You dictated our strife,

our separation, my jealousy, my guarded love, and you even created this, our eternal bargain.

Two straws were held out over an empty gap in time, January 8th, 1935, and you, brother Elvis, drew the shorter. And I know, you were never certain who got the better deal.

I, Jesse Aron, your stillborn twin brother buried in Priceville Cemetery, or you, the great Elvis Presley.

But all along brother, I had all the life I needed, just living through you.

Somehow I still feel that there were words I should've said, some meaning left to be translated in those last moments before your birth, and thirty minutes later I was gone.

If I could've spoken to you then, how I would've confided in you. But I stayed silent.

Oh, the things I could've said.

Back on that day, when we two went our separate ways.

Elvis' Dog

LAVONNE MUELLER

I first saw the Presley litter on Alabama Street
there was four of them
mewing, yipping in a $50 a month apartment
oatmeal paper on the walls
Grandma Minnie Mae
Gladys
Vernon
Elvis

Gladys threw fist-size biscuits from the stove
for a human, Elvis could really fetch

Grandma Minnie Mae
held up red-flannel-hash
to see who could grab it first

Elvis was hard running
with a good nose

after he was let out of Humes High School every day
we'd take to the rut roads and creek
all the gone-to-brush backyards
    near the Marl Metal Manufacturing Company
    where Elvis earned extra money
        on the night shift

I worried his old shoes with my teeth

he bonded me

spit into my throat
    his thick saliva made us brothers

I would wiggle my hind-end hard
without embarrassment
(I hold lapdogs in contempt)

you won't find me
on any veterinarian's door chart

Elvis with his guitar
wind turning our ears backwards
me chasing after day-squirrels
then
I'd stop
howl into the goldenrods and grass
Elvis behind me locked on point
his eyes strained
his nose quivering
knowing he was hearing a good sound
listening
like he always done
at
gospel group sings
Red's Place
Silver Stallion Nightclub on Union Street
Eagle's Nest on Lamar Avenue

now
listening hard
to
raw, rocking howling
mostly mongrel
hot with a little Blackwood Brothers
dangerous from the Harmonizing Four
shaking like the Soul Stirrers

Dinah
Fats
Leroy Car
T-Bone Walker
Bukka White
Rufus Thomas
Louis Jordan
Big Ma Rainey
Sonny Boy Williamson
B. B. King
Ukulele Ike

bluebirds on the tree branches
crying for their babies
washed away by the storm

roots
breathing in the dark
white violets
yearning for their bees
this whole marshland of Memphis
played out like WDIA Radio

and me
teaching Elvis to unbutton singing

in all that soapweed and blue joint grass
smeared with swells of wet dirt
stone bruised
the sun sinking into my footsteps

me
shaking off bull thistles and skunk cabbage
afraid of feelings not meant for dwarf spruce and brambles
this hound dog
got up to high D
and kept it there to make a King.

All Shook Up

FRANK HIGGINS

LONNIE: Well, sir, Elvis did a concert in Louisville one time,
and I wanted good seats, y' know.
And so, tickets went on sale at eight in the morning
but I wanted good seats so I took off school
to drive up the day before
cuz I was going to camp out overnight
at the ticket window.
Well, I was driving this guy's Trans Am
that I was testing the transmission for,
but the transmission tore up
and I had to get towed on I-64 to an all-night station.
Well, Lexington is bad for Trans Am parts at night,
so I slept in the car, and by the time I got fixed
I didn't make Louisville till ten the next morning.

Well, there were people who camped outside ten days
for tickets. Slept out in the rain.
So I knew my seats would be bad.
But when the concert came, my seats are *behind* the stage.
And there's a sign, "Elvis Presley will not turn around."
But during the show, Elvis turned around two or three times
and did the whole song to us.

He came to a stop, and Elvis said,
"I understand there's a girl with leukemia
who slept out twelve days to get the first ticket."
And Elvis brought her up there onstage,
and she said her name was Sally.
And Elvis gave her two free tickets

99

for the next show in St. Louis
and said he'd fly her there and her guest on his plane,
the *Lisa-Marie.*
And the girl broke down and cried and said
she'd never been out of Kentucky her whole life,
and Elvis kept her there onstage with him,
and he held her and sang his song "If I Can Dream."
. . . Elvis was . . . you know . . . .

He was just . . . .
. . . and I left the arena, drove all night back to Quicksand,
and do you know that whole drive in the dark
I never said one word, never played the radio.
Got home, went to bed. Cried.

Thinkin' of Takin' Care of Business

TAD CURRY

Young man, late twenties, slim. College-educated, but with the attitude of a blue-collar worker. Dressed in old blue jeans, black boots, and work shirt. He is not overly emotional, but he is honest. He speaks.

I'm not really sure why I got an Elvis tattoo, or any tattoo, for that matter. I didn't even like tattoos until my house-mates all got them; then I was jealous. I wasn't an Elvis fan, either, until I went to Graceland a couple of months ago. I swear I was only going so I could laugh at the people who go to Graceland—the "Elvis Lives" freaks, the ones who line the gates of Graceland in an all-night vigil on the anniversary of the King's death, hoping, almost expecting, he'll show up and sing "That's All Right," and everything will be all right. I just wanted to gawk at the gawkers. But there's no way to walk away from Graceland an impartial Elvis observer. He gets inside some part of you, for better or for worse, and you can't help but appreciate him, at the very least, as the first and greatest of that late twentieth-century breed, the Global Superstar. You're likely to feel more like Elvis was the friend you didn't know well enough, whose gentle heart quit before its time. If you say you're unaffected by Graceland, you're either jaded and cynical beyond hope of redemption or a liar.

I left Graceland knowing that it wasn't Elvis' fault. It wasn't his fault that he made bad movies, that he got fat and lazy on stage, that his money was managed right out from under him; wasn't his fault that he got addicted to prescription drugs, that he had a heart attack while sitting on the porcelain throne and died face down in the shag carpeting of his bathroom. If he was the first Superstar, he was also the first Victim, with a capital V. I knew, after Graceland, that Colonel Parker ruled his movie career in the sixties with an iron hand, forcing him into lousy script after lousy script. And Parker took advantage of the young heart-singer's naïveté, contracting for himself 50 percent of the star's earnings while dealing on the side for any dime he could stuff in his tight pockets. Elvis' father, Vernon, a man who quit school before eighth grade, ruined his estate by letting the IRS calculate his taxes. I'm no financial wizard—otherwise I wouldn't be delivering paint for a living—but I do know that you let anyone but the IRS decide how much you owe the government. And the Memphis Mafia, the band of cronies that were with Elvis from his army days until the day he was put in the ground, hung on his coattails until Elvis couldn't stand up on his own; they picked his pockets until the coffin closed on their fingertips. Elvis was the good guy through all of this, performing for the love of his music, his fans, and his Lord. That's what I thought when I left Graceland, anyway. (*Pause*)

Like I said, a month ago I saw my roommates' tattoos and got jealous. Up until then, I still thought like every middle-class mother in America did—a tattoo is forever; the design better be one you won't hate in three years, or even three months. But mostly I couldn't think of a design that was worth spending fifty bucks on. My housemates' tattoos, though, got me thinking, and I was still high on Graceland. . . . (*Short pause*)

The Memphis Mafia was Elvis' official title for his boys. They remind me, as a group, of that Chihuahua in the Warner Brothers cartoon that just dances around and around Spike, the big bulldog, asking him, "What're we gonna do today, huh, Spike? What, huh?" And Elvis never told them to "Shaddap." I don't know, because I wasn't even born yet, but I think he really did need them around him, or he at least wanted them around for a while, and he needed them to be official. I read that he tried to give them uniforms, making them wear black jumpsuits, but that was before stretch fabrics came around, and I guess their crotches kept splitting. So the uniform got reduced to a logo—the letters TCB with a lightning bolt shooting down below the C. It stood for Takin' Care of Business in a Flash. Elvis had rings and pendants made up, and all the boys, and whoever else was authorized by Elvis, wore them. They really did take care of business in a flash, thought most of their business seemed to involve getting Elvis what and whom he wanted—namely, young, eager, female fans—and keeping away what and whom he didn't want. For this gopher status they got a salary and free room and board for more than fifteen years. And some cool jewelry.

TCB in a Flash—that's the tattoo I got. Here it is.

He frees his left arm from his shirt, revealing a tattoo, like the logo described, just below the shoulder.

Folks seem to agree that it was worth the money. I think it's a cool design, but I'm not sure if it's accurate. I mean, I wonder if Takin' Care of Business in a Flash really applies to me, because I can't seem to take care of anything in a flash. I can hold a job, and I give my best when other people depend on my work, but, hell, I'm a delivery boy. I graduated *cum laude* from college with degrees in History and Classics. I should be translating Juvenal's satires and critiquing revisionist history books, but instead I drive cans of paint all over the tristate area. Not that I'd be writing history books and translating defunct languages if I weren't driving all day—I don't really want to spend my life in academia; there's no action there—

but I'd like to be doing *something* creative. As it is, I wake up, my boss tells me what to deliver where and in what order, I drive, I go home, I sleep. The most creative decisions I get to make are what roads to take to avoid traffic and construction, and where to eat lunch. It's solid work, I guess, and it keeps me from getting soft, but my mind is turning to jelly. As far as the Memphis Mafia is concerned, I'm probably taking more-than-adequate care of business, but I aspire to compare myself to TCBers who are more than water-schlepps and salaried pimps.

I want to take care of business like Elvis could have if he tried, but didn't. He went way soft in the mid sixties, when he was making such riveting cinematic experiences as "Clambake" and "Spinout." He must have felt like a sort of delivery boy, getting instructions from Hollywood about which version of the same hackneyed formula he was to deliver this time around. If Elvis had stopped for even a second to look at how his life was being run, he'd have realized just that: he wasn't running his life; it was being run for him. And badly, with the greedy Colonel Parker, the ill-equipped Vernon, and the yes-men of the Mafia in charge. The King seemed content to just coast along through the decade, not taking responsibility for anything except his leisure time. When he wasn't filming, he was sitting around on vacation in Hawaii or Palm Springs until the next movie rolled in off the assembly line. And even then, he only took action because he was contracted, because someone told him it was time to make the movie. Personal Initiative, Creative Drive: ZERO. Goose egg. Zilch. He broke out of that in '68 and '69, when he did the live *Elvis* TV special and recorded the Memphis albums. Man, those had some rockers—"Suspicious Minds," "Kentucky Rain," and "Long Black Limousine." It seemed like he was finally going to live for himself, creating what he wanted to create and answering to himself, but then he retreated again, this time to years of identical concert tours in Vegas and arenas across the country—different formula from the movies, but pure formula nonetheless. (*Pause*)

I'm not saying I have the talent that Elvis had. We aren't even comparable as far as talent in our respective fields. And I guess there's the difference: I don't even have a field of creative expertise. I don't know what I want to do with my life. I know what I don't want, and I know I want to create something, but I have no drive to figure out what that creation will be. I think about it a lot, when I'm driving and when I'm sitting at home, but it never gets beyond curious speculation. That's the worst part—I'm just too lazy to do anything about it. I am clearly undeserving of the TCB mantle . . . even though I think I'm no less worthy than the Memphis Mafia. (*Pause*)

At least I'm thinking about what I want to do. I don't doubt that Elvis was itching to get back to rock and roll after Hollywood. But any ideas he had were probably smothered by the Colonel's weighty presence. And though it was good for his career to get back to performing live, the formula his tours fell into must have seemed equally stifling. And if he was entertaining thoughts in the mid seventies of a comeback from his comeback, he died before he could act. Or maybe he was taking action when he died—self-destruction is one way of taking control of your life.

Self-destruction. I guess I could blame anyone I wanted to for Elvis' decline, but he was the one who got addicted to prescription drugs; he was the one who dieted on deep-fried peanut butter-and-banana sandwiches, burgers, and shakes; he was the one who gave up on himself. And it's no one's fault but my own that I sit around whining about not knowing what to do with my life. There's no one to sue for my own inaction.

The time comes in a guy's life when he either sits down and delivers paint for the rest of his life, or he stands up, shakes his hips, and takes care of business in a flash. I'm tired of delivering paint. And I have the stupid logo etched permanently into my skin, so I might as well live up to it.

Elvis' First Bike

KAREN De WITT

You ain't never seen nothing like it. I come out here just to
have another look. Not that I ain't looked at it near everyday
since they put it up in the Tupelo Hardware. Right smack up
there in the center. Just like it's ona stage. Just like me in that
contest last year. I stand on a chair and sang "Old Shep" just
like I do at home and they give me second prize. Five dollars
and I got to go on all the rides at the fair, for free. Was broad-
cast all over WELO Radio. All over Mississippi and Alabama
and Tennessee and everywhere. Heck, wann't nothing.
Wann't nothing to having a Western Flyer like I'ma have now.
Look at her up there. Right up there among the hammers
and saws and big rolls a wire. Fine as she want to be. Red and
shiny as a apple. That guard's shaped just like Flash Gordon's
spaceship. And that seat is real leather. Humph. I'ma put red
and white streamers in the handles like Marley Wilson back
in Biloxi. I'ma put a baseball card in them spokes, too.
Brrrraaccck, brrraccck, brraacck. It's gonna sound real loud
when I ride down 'em streets. I'ma put saddlebags on the side
just like Trigger's got.

They gonna buy it today. I just know it. They been
knowing I want that bike since last Christmas. I didn't get it
then, but they been saving. They got a cigar box up in the
closet. And I just know it's got that $29.95 for my Western
Flyer. They promised, you know. And my Pa's been working
real steady now since we moved from Biloxi. And we all living together, too. Me and my Pa and Mamma and my aunts
and my grandmaw. I been prayering real hard, too. Elder Tate
say that if you ask you shall receive. He said it's like grace.
You say grace and then you get to eat the food. Well, I been

asking, see, and last time we had a meeting, I felt all tingly and know that the Spirit was answering me. Nah, I didn't get the spirit that knocks you down, so you rocking and rolling on the floor like Miss Kittles done last camp meeting. Lord, she was funny, bucking on the floor. No, I just felt my heart kinna break and I knew this time I'ma get it.

See my Pa's in there now. That's him leaning on the counter, jawing with Mr. Lamar. He look serious 'cause that's how you do when you jewing. Gonna buy it any minute. My Mamma's over there. She looking at all a them things folk brought in for pawn. Mr. Lamar give you cash money for something and give it right back when you bring the money in. But he get to keep it if you don't. That's how it work. That's why they got all them things in there. Radios and shaving kits and harmonicas and things. My Mamma's looking at a gittar right now, see. Any minute she gonna call me. Then they gonna take that bike otta the window and I'ma ride it right down the street. Brand-new. I'ma ride at night, too. That Western Flyer, it got a light, right up there in front. Like a rocket. And a bell. It gotta bell, too. Right there on the side of the handlebar. Can't wait to ring that bell. I'ma shine that bike up so good and I'm love that bike tenderly.

In the Year
Twenty Twenty-Seven

MARGARET HUNT AND RICHARD HOLODY

Gladys, 22, white, a blue-collar girl from Memphis. She is intel-
ligent and very earnest. She wears Star Treklike clothes, but with
anachronistic touches, like her Elvis pin and black cat's eye glasses
from the fifties. The time is January 8, 2027. The place is
Graceland, the director's office.

GLADYS: Elvis woulda been ninety-two today, and I'm twenty-
two. Yessuh . . . That, in a nutshell, is why I'm perfect for this
job . . . Whew, I'll try, but, Mr. Parker—I gotta tell ya, on my
way over this morning—on the Tri-State Zipper—I kept
thinking: Gladys, just put it in a nutshell and he'll hire you!
. . . And I just done that and you . . . you ain't—I gotta ask!
I'm sorry. You related to, you know, Colonel? . . .

(*Disappointed*) Oh, well, the world can only live with so
many coincidences, I guess. . . .

Okay, then. Hard to know where to begin when there's so
much. To begin with, we have the same birthday. Bet you
don't get many people applying who can say that, huh? . . .

(*Surprised*) Oh, my . . . Well, you probably know my
mother Marie-Lisa, 'cause she just retired . . . Oh, well, I knew
you were new, but I—oh, right, I was saying, uh . . . What
you probably don't know is that my Gram was hired as a tour
guide the very first day! The day Graceland opened! An original! Actually, she's an original in more ways than one. (*Laughs*)

Yessuh . . . I'm getting to my qualifications. I'm just
kinda sneaking up on 'em. It's just all connected, you know?
Like, you know, uh, this is the twenty-first consecutive birth-

day that I have celebrated here at Graceland. Exceptin' only the day my momma was in the hospital with me, on do you believe it, Elvis' birthday!

You know she had this feeling it would happen on that day. Even had a plan to drive to Tupelo! But daddy nixed that. "The only thing good about the hospitals in Tennessee is that they ain't in Mississippi!" We called him "Vernon" as a joke, though he never laughed at it much.

Anyways, long story short, twenty-one straight birthdays.

Momma said I loved it the first time, too. Don't remember that, course. First thing I remember was hearing gospel music. Wasn't till I went on the net to school that I found out not all white people listened to gospel so much as we did. But momma said, "You love Elvis, ya gotta love what Elvis loved." So, no hip-hop, no frazz, no bubba rock for me—gospel. In high school, they thought I was a little digital, me and my Elvis. But when you got the best America ever offered, you're just wasting the precious time that God gave you listening to anybody else . . . What?

Right, right, qualifications. I know Graceland like the back of my hand. Where the gold records from Norway are. Why the gold Rolls Royce ain't here. Where he kept his favorite Mario Lanza records. Name it, know it. . . . No suh. That's my best qualification!

I seen the changes here. . . . Oh, no! Not in Graceland. Graceland never changes! Nah. I mean changes in the people who come to pay their respects to Elvis. The tourists, though they never seemed like tourists to me.

Gram says I shoulda been here when when it opened. She'd say, "Gladys, they were all my age!" Momma said that, too. "It was better then, Gladys. What's happening now? Where's the people my age?" I used to think, they're still here. I couldn't figure what they were telling me that was different.

But, then, I guess I grew up, and started to realize that the visitors were their ages—Gram's age, more or less, in the 1980s, Momma's age in the '90s and oughts. 'Cause they were younger, which is hard for a kid to figure out. Today, what I see is old people. I don't know if you want to talk about this, Mr. Parker, but, you know, *those* people—the ones who don't seem to know who Elvis is. Who . . . laugh.

The best thing about Graceland is that it's about the best of Elvis. Sure, he had bad times. Who doesn't? It's like the country—there's wars, depressions, that terrible California sinkhole thing, but where'd you rather live? . . . What's important is his sweetness. How happy he was making people feel so good just to hear this one boy sing. That he sang rock-and-roll, R&B, gospel, down-home, Delta, heartland country—in the same song! If that ain't America, well then I've wasted my life barking at the wrong tree! . . .

That's another nutshell. I can bring them back for you, Mr. Parker. I can! Absolutely! I can bring back the days when the parking lots would have licenses from every one of the fifty-four states on the same day. The days when you didn't have to advertise, because every American knew in their bones that coming to Graceland was as American as standing at attention at the start of a ballgame in the Wrigley Dome. I can explain, to the people my age, who Elvis is. Nobody seems to be able to do that anymore! . . .

What? . . . Oh, no, Mr.—Oh, my God! That's a crying shame, Mr. Parker. I had a feeling times were tough, but you just can't make Graceland *virtual!* . . . Elvis is reality! Please! I'll work for—okay, okay . . . You just don't know! People don't know any more. And that's a crying shame.

My Book Report

MURRAY HORWITZ

Lights up on Randy, an eight-year-old. The actor playing Randy may be of any race or sex. Randy reads from a paper he is holding.

RANDY: Hello, I am Randy Thalmus. The title of my biography is *Elvis, the Man and the King* by Sora Templeton. It is published by Little Panther Books. It was published in 1995.

Elvis Presley was a singer and actor and guitar player. You probably have heard of him. He is called The King of Rock 'n' Roll, or sometimes just the King.

Elvis Presley was born in (*Randy has difficulty with the name*) Tupelo, Mississippi, on January 8, 1935. His family was poor but Elvis liked to sing. When he was thirteen years old, they moved to Memphis, Tennessee, where Elvis drove a truck. He liked to listen to the music of African American people.

One day, he saw a sign for a record company, and paid four dollars to make a record for his mother. Elvis did not like the record. But the people at the record company called him to sing another song. When he sang his African American music, they liked it.

Soon, Elvis was a big star. He had many hit records, such as "Don't Be Cruel," "Heartbreak Hotel," and "You Ain't—" (*Randy hesitates*) "You Aren't Anything But a Hound Dog."

Wherever he went, people screamed and cheered for him. He was handsome and people liked the way he sang. But some people did not like him and did not like the way he sang. One newspaper said he was vulgar, which I had to look up. It means not having good manners. When he was on TV, they would only show his face, so people could not see him shaking. This is called censorship.

Elvis Presley made a lot of movies and became a great actor, but in 1958 he had to go into the Army. When he got out he was worried that he wouldn't still be a big star, but he was.

Randy looks up from the paper.

He was still a big star.

Randy resumes reading.

But he started having problems. He was married to a woman named Priscilla, who left him for a karate instructor, even though Elvis was more famous than the karate instructor. He became fatter and he started taking drugs.

In 1977, Elvis was having a nice time with some friends at his house, called Graceland, and went to bed. During the night, he had a heart attack and died. He was forty-two years old. His mother also died of a heart attack when she was forty-two, so maybe it wasn't the drugs.

Some people think Elvis Presley is still alive, and that they see him. One woman said she saw him in a Burger King in Michigan in 1988, but I don't think so, because my Grandma died over a year ago, and even though my Grandpa still talks to her, I know she's dead.

Why I think you should read this book is because it is interesting, and you will learn many things about Elvis Presley and about African Americans.

Why I think Elvis Presley is important is because he made a lot of people happy and he was a big star.

I do think he is a hero, because he fought censorship, which is bad, and because Ed Sullivan, who was a big TV star, told everybody he was really a nice person. I also liked it that he wanted to make a record for his mom.

Elvis Presley is not a good example for young people to follow, because he used drugs, and because everybody says he had something special that nobody can (*Randy has difficulty with the word*) imitate.

Things I think Elvis Presley should have done differently are I think he should not have taken drugs and he should not have been the King, because we learned in Social Studies that they did not want a king when they made the United States. Some people wanted George Washington to be king, but he refused. I think if George Washington would not be king, Elvis Presley shouldn't either.

Thank you for paying attention, and are there any questions?

Lights fade out.

Shocking Secrets About Elvis Revealed in Agonizing True-Life Confessions of Longtime Fan

MICHAEL WRIGHT

Lyla enters. We're in her living room. She's wearing a tight, fuzzy sweater, and Capri pants with gold midheel sandals—looking very much like the classic Elvis girlfriend from the movies, though at least twenty years too far on. She's got something to tell us, but she's not quite ready to get to it. She sits and takes a moment to get comfy. She lights a cigarette, takes a sip from her coffee cup.

LYLA: I just love the way cigarettes and coffee go together, don't you? It's like—liquid butter turning into air or something. I like the way they kind of grab my chest: take that puff, sip a little sip, and you get a kind of a breathless, fluttery feeling, now don't you? Like first love.

She smiles at herself. Looks to us to see how we're receiving this. Finding us not too judgmental, she relaxes a little.

I mean, OK, I know I shouldn't do any of this stuff any more, but it's my life isn't it? And I know some of y'all are concerned about that old hand-me-down smoke and such, but this *is* MY house. (*She smiles again to say: that wasn't meant to be mean, but a fact is a fact*)

Anyway, let me not go on and on here; y'all didn't come here to listen to my personal philosophizin' about what-all. Let me just get to it? (*A moment*)

This may be the hardest thing I've ever had to do, but I am, effective today, officially resigning as President-for-Life of the Elvis Presley Fan Club of Okmulgee, Oklahoma. I do not do this because I want to but because I must. Because I have carried a burden in my heart all these many years and must now confess the truth to you before my secret rots out my heart like a termite sucking the guts out of a two-by-four. (*Another moment as she composes herself*)

OK. I did it. (*Beat*) I killed Elvis. (*Beat*) That's about the reaction I expected. Oh, I can read your faces all right: skepticism, disbelief, out-and-out "she's crazier than a rocking chair." Well, that's fine, it's about what I expected, although I guess I thought some of y'all *serious* fan club members would be more welcoming to the plain truth. Well, fine: you doubting Tammys out there can leave if you want—and Earl there—but I'm going to tell the whole story so make it quick if you're going so I can get on with it.

She lights another cigarette. Evidently no one has gotten up.

Well, there now. As Reverend Collard always says: there's nothing you can say to a true believer. (*Beat*) A long time ago in the late fifties, when I was a young thing, and boys liked me a whole lot, I was seeing a guy named Butch. Butch was a guitar-playin' boy from my high school, and he was in a rock and roll band that was real popular around here. Some of you might remember that band: The DA's? It was named for what they called the haircuts the guys wore where they had that kind of waterfall in the front over their foreheads, and the sides combed way around to meet in the back? And the little part that kind of came down in a point on their neck was called a duck's ass: D. A. Not to be confused with the one in the law area, although I often wonder. (*She laughs*)

Anyway, Butch was the rhythm guitar player; a very quiet type until you were alone with him, if you know what I mean. And Butch was coming around my house all the time and one night my parents were out, and it was just me and him in the club cellar with a stack of forty-fives on the record player. And, well, I told Butch on the first date: "I bite tongues, mister." And, after a couple of slaps, he respected that—kept his hands to himself and what-all. But there we were, alone, and outside it was June and you could smell the night through the screen windows, and I was just thinking how I might like Butch to hold me a little closer when "Love Me Tender" came on the record player and before I knew it we were dancing—but Butch was holding me practically at arm's length and I'm thinking: I didn't want you to listen to me THIS good—Ladies, I think you all know what I mean here—you, too, Earl—and I remember wishing Butch could just be a whole lot less like Butch and more like, well, like Elvis. . . . (*Beat*) And that's when it happened. I looked at Butch and his little thin lips had got all full and even had a curly little sneer in them, and his eyes were all dark and smoky, and—well, things followed things, but the whole time I knew something way down deep: I had called Elvis forth and He'd come unto me. In Butch. (*Beat. After a moment, she pulls herself up out of the reverie*) And from that time on, He has come to me in so many other men. (*Beat*) That didn't come out right. I don't mean so many other men like it was with Butch. I just mean I would just find myself thinking of Him in the supermarket, even, and the guy at the meat counter would be looking out at me through His eyes, or the cop directing traffic downtown would suddenly do that kind of leg shift He used, you know? I would call Elvis unto me— sometimes without even thinking about it—and He would just . . . *manifest.*

She shivers, then shifts forward in her seat.

Well, after years of this, I finally thought: why am I drinking champagne out of Co-cola bottles? Why don't I just go get me the real thing Himself? So I started saving up so I could go see Him perform—and wouldn't you know it? That's exactly when He stopped doing shows. (*Pause*) At first, I was real depressed. I thought it was a rejection: Him saying to me "don't come." But then I understood: I was being tested. I was being asked: Was I Elvis-worthy or just another fan—no offense, y'all—but was I truly . . . worthy?

She takes a nervous sip of coffee.

Well, obviously, I wanted to be Elvis-worthy, or what point would it all have? So, right then and there I took a pledge: I would make myself into the very definition of the true—tru*est*—believer that I could. I would be worthy. Or die. (*This calls for another cigarette*)

I spent the next year reading and re-reading every book and magazine article I could find, seeing all of His movies I could track down—this is *before* video, young people, so I did me some driving—and listening to all His albums again and again, wearing them out and buying new ones, and then one day I was sitting on the floor, listening to "Heartbreak Hotel"—writing a poem for His birthday using the letters of His name to start each line?—when it hit me like a ton of frozen turkeys. I was preparing, that was true. But preparing for what? I laid back right there on the floor and I begged Him for guidance, and I looked deep into my own heart, and eventually the answer came clear as a bell: You must be more than worthy; you must be His ideal woman. Yes. (*Beat. She closes her eyes, reliving*)

This is when I took all that I'd done already and got real scientific about it—because now I had a mission. I went back through all those movies and got a profile of His ideal woman by combining all the women into one. I covered my walls with charts of every conceivable fact I could lay my fingers on. And that's when I realized I was *that* close but for one or two details. Per example: His truest like was for blondes—they were in the majority—and I was brunette.

Then. And, He liked blue eye shadow—well, those were easy—I didn't see how peroxide and Maybelline were going to make me ideal. I went through my lists and charts again and again, and found that I matched up in every way—after going blonde—except one. Except one! And when I saw it, it was like all the great discoveries: it was simple—He liked a real hourglass figure. I had the ideal hip and the bust size—sorry, Earl—but thanks to a long line of ancestors from places I can't even pronounce, I had the kind of waistline that made me more the shape of a clock than an hourglass. (*She laughs*)

So I saved. I saved and I saved, and after two years I had enough money to do it. And when my Momma, bless her heart, begged me not to do it, I just said: Adam gave up his for Eve; it's the least *I* can do for Elvis. And so I had the operation. Even now you can still see the results.

She poses a little for us, showing off her slender waist.

And, lo, I was ready to walk the last mile. (*Sip of coffee*)

And after the six months I spent healing up and learning how to breathe with tighter and tighter cinchers, and taking voice lessons so I could sing the occasional duet with Him on our TV specials, and practicing my first greetings to Him day after day after day—I. WAS. READY. I was worthy, I was—ideal. Elvis-ideal. (*Beat; she smiles*)

And don't you know? That's just when He began to perform live again? Every sign pointed the way. And I didn't care that He had plumped up like a loaf of bread, I built up my money once again, and set my sights on His next appearance, and I was ready. (*Another cigarette. This is the home stretch, and she's gearing up for it*)

And so, I flew out, I checked in, and I made ready. I went a day early to be sure everything was in place, and I did not step one foot outside my room to keep from distracting myself in any way, shape, or form. On the night of the performance, I was there and ready: front row, center. (*Beat*)

I wore my raincoat over my outfit, and kept it on. I was ready and I was biding my time for *my* moment. When He came out, I felt the love sweep over me like a tornado, and I could feel His eyes on me from time to time, but I waited. I could feel myself aching to be welcomed by Him to the stage and held in His now-burly arms in front of everyone, but I waited. I was dying to bury my face in His glorious and bountiful flesh—but I waited. (*Beat*) And then He got there—like I knew He would, in time, taking His time, teasing me with other songs—He got to "Love Me Tender," the song that started it all . . . (*Beat; she stands. Light grows around her*)

My heart is louder than the band as I slip my coat off carefully in my seat, not wanting to appear too eager—or uncoordinated—and just at the moment when the song is reaching its greatest intensity, I stand up, and let Him take me in. I can feel His perfect eyes moving up and down me, measuring my body with his eyes, checking out the colors of my outfit, and I don't care who behind me is saying "Sit down," I just let Him know me as I had made myself to be known by Him. (*Beat*)

And then . . . And then, His eyes flicker off in a different direction for a moment, come back to me and then return to the other direction, and I look back to where He's looking and see another blonde on the aisle with blue eye shadow and the ideal dimensions and I think: what could it be, what has she got that I have not? We look the same age, nearly the same height, and well, maybe her waist is a half-inch smaller than mine, but this would be minutia beyond belief and that's when I see what it is. (*A pause; she tries to compose herself a bit*)

Everything on her is—(*She can barely bring herself to say it*)—FOOD! *Her* blonde hair is a bouffant of meringue; *her* fuzzy sweater is a coating of coconut flakes layered on top of a delectable paste of almonds combined with a cream cheese and butter icing, and *her* skirt is made of a potpourri of flavored pastas, while the pattern on the skirt is made of bite-sized selections of all his favorite foods. I can't see her feet, but I have the feeling her boots are made of licorice. And I am all set to yell at Him: I can be a buffet, too, my King, I truly can, a smorgasbord!—when I see him hesitate, and His eyes come back to me because He knows I am the superior one, and at that moment she knows she has lost Him but she cries out "Elvis!" and He looks at her and I look and I see her lift her hand in His direction, and bite off a finger tip and offer it unto Him. (*Pause*) And He holds his Hand unto her. (*Pause*) And the woman rises up, and walks along the shoulders of the crowd—and now I see: her boots are made of pralines; Lord, pralines, who could compete?—and she meets Him on the stage—and He eats her fingertip and part of an ear after licking her meringue hair—and Dr. Pepper is spouting from her breasts—and I know then it is all over for me. (*She holds herself together, barely*)

And that's when I turned my back. On Him. On it. On just about everything that meant anything in my life, but I had the will to do it then, the strength, to turn away and walk through that crowd into the rest of my life. (*Beat*) And, you know, He didn't say a single thing? Oh, I could tell He was having some feelings; I could hear the little catch in His voice just as He sang "—all my dreams come true—" right on the word *dreams,* there it was, this little dry patch in His soul his voice could not go past, but that was all. Even when He had a last chance to redeem Himself—to call me back— He wouldn't do it. In the end, He became the gross by-product of what He'd been His whole life—which was unspeakable, unquenchable desire; but in the end he was only . . . appetite. (*Beat. Another cigarette*)

And I turned my prayers around after that. I had summoned Him, and I believed I could send Him away. I prayed without ceasing, night and day, for His own appetite to consume Him. And it did. Just a few months later, He was dead. And everybody was speculating and tongue wagging about it, but I knew what was what. And now you do, too. (*Beat*) And

I'm not sorry. I want that to be clear to everybody. I. Am. Not. Sorry. (*Beat*) I only regret being untruthful to y'all—and that I wasn't listening all those years and years, when the clue to his deep, dark secret was there the whole time? Why hadn't I heard it when it was so obvious right from the get-go?

She stands, ready to go.

What's that, Earl? It's not obvious to you? Well, then listen, darlin', 'cause here it comes this once, the secret: "Love Me . . . (*She mimes biting her finger*) Tender*"?

The lights begin a slow fade. Lyla collects her stuff and slowly moves off. "Love Me Tender" fades up as she exits.

Our Elvis

BILL EVANS

Fat mechanic with thick sideburns
and carefully combed back, jump-back hair.
Satin kind of pajama suit,
rhinestony as a galaxy! Here in this
funky, country bar, where we have
escaped. O Rockabilly Hideaway!
Saturday, late, while the last
paycheck dances. And you city folk think
Rednecks don't know how to Swing . . .

This afternoon, this guy, he
fixed my car. And tonight,
tonight, he's a fucking star!
Light-years more living
than the original.
He's a fake,
but who isn't?

I never got to see the real one,
the famous one,
the King
one, the dead one, the
kidnapped by
aliens one,
the pill
head one,
the one who roams
the stellar
mojo incognito,

the one I read about
breathlessly in
supermarket check-out lines,
recorder of my favorite spaced-out Christmas tune:

    Merry Christmas, baby/
    You sure do treat me right. Etc.
    Bought me a diamond ring for Christmas/
    Now I'm livin' in Paradise. Etc.

White Negro
mama's boy
blues thief
Graceland
immortal
Rock and Roll
icon demigod
cracker heartthrob
with a taste for
jailbait and a Voice.

Whose effective persona
focused public attention
on the physical arena of
hot teen-age sexuality.

Quite a threat to authority
and patriarchal masculinity
masked as musical commodity
stressing action and relation.

I mean, the subtext of
DOING IT
versus
OWNING IT.
A very dangerous

addition to bourgeois pop culture
from the war
rooms of the poor . . .

And shit, *that* Elvis
wouldn't touch my car.
We'd still be stuck
in the rain,
afar . . .
Full electrical
spark plug
burn out/
Pottstown,
Pennsylvania
1990 something—
Kiwi shoe polish
Mrs. Smith's pies,
former methamphetamine capital
of the Eastern seaboard,
there to visit Grandma
and Grandpa McWharter,
very near the end of our century, the Twentieth,
North American international
info-technological
televisional metaphysical Christian evangelical
theoretical magical financial empire, U. S. of A.

Where I, uhh,
reside and
reluctantly travel.

Culture Warrior
school of
realistic
anecdotalism.

Offer my
report,
another
big-mouth try.

And wave
a giant,
anecdotal,
Cult-War hi
to his highness,
Clyde "Little Elvis" Monroe,

of Monroe and Monroe

Towing and Repair—

hero of
this poem,
right
now and forever,

blasting
his secular
self mic-ward,

elder brother
to Ezekiel
Monroe on
saxophone,

the fabulous Monroe
sisters,
Gina
and
Angela,

assorted
cousin
Monroes
bashing
various
percussives,

and, golly, dear
audience,

and heck,
everybody!

Whose HEARTBREAK HOTEL
is a
radical
miracle.

I'm telling you.

Love Me Tender

MICHAEL KEARNS

Elvis is twentyish and possesses an oddball charisma.

ELVIS: Elvis died of AIDS. Swear to God. Scout's honor. Cross my heart and hope to—no, I don't. How do I know? I am— it's the God's truth—the reincarnation of Elvis Presley. Me, who used to be known as little Herbie Lucas of St. Louis, Missouri; I am known on these streets by one name only: Elvis.

Clift advised me to change my name. That day we met on Hollywood Boulevard, smack-dab on top of Elvis' star, he tole me that everybody who comes to Hollywood changes their name. He changed his to Clift Montgomery—from what, he never told me.

I'd just arrived from St. Louis. Walked from the bus station on Vine to the King's star at Hollywood and Highland. Clift was standin' there. Not exactly standin'; he didn't jus' stand, he posed. He had on some sorta long, black cape— even though it was the middle of August. August 17, to be exact: the anniversary of Elvis' death. Same day as my birth-day. Clift's hair was dyed black as coal—like Elvis'—and he had black makeup smeared on his long eyelashes.

I introduced myself—"Herbie Lucas from St. Louis"— and that's when he said I should change my name because he could immediately see I was "blessed with star quality."

When I told him it was my birthday, he nearly flipped. He started flappin' his hands as he spoke; he looked like he was gonna take flight. "Child," he said. "You are special. We'll name you . . ." At this moment, he looked down at the King's star, real dramatic-like, and shouted, "Elvis!"

It was the first time—since my Mama died when I was nine years old—anyone ever tole me I was special. My Mama thought I was special 'cause I won a talent context doin' an Elvis impersonation when I was seven years old. I mouthed the words to "You Ain't Nothin' But a Hound Dog" and rotated my hips. The last thing my Mama said to me, on her deathbed, was, "Son, you are special. One day you're gonna be a big star like Elvis."

I had no daddy, period. When Mama died, I was tossed in one foster home after another; no one told me I was special. I promised myself to get to Hollywood by my sixteenth birthday—even if it meant runnin' away. Not so's anyone would notice; there was thirteen other kids in the last place I lived.

Clift was the best thing ever happened to me. Since winnin' that contest.

"Sweet sixteen," he said, all excited. After taking a buncha pictures of me by Elvis' star, Clift invited me to dinner at the Snow White Cafe. We sat under a window box fulla plastic flowers and a painting of one of the dwarfs, like he was lookin' outta the window. I think it was Doc. There was a buncha young boys hangin' out in the restaurant—Clift jokingly called them "Grumpy" and "Sleepy" and "Horny."

Clift told me he was a photographer, a past-life analyst, and a personal manager. He said it wasn't unusual for people in Hollywood to have more than one occupation. He also waited tables the the Hamburger Hamlet, across the street from Grauman's Chinese.

He offered to let me stay at his place on Wilcox, within walkin' distance of Elvis' star: the very apartment building where Auntie Em, from *The Wizard of Oz,* committed suicide. She got all dolled up, with her makeup on and everything and put a plastic bag over her head. Clift was fulla stories like that one—'bout movie stars and how they died.

Clift knew a lot about fate and destiny. He said we were meant to be together since what I needed most was photographs, past-life therapy, and a manager—not to mention a free hamburger at the Hamlet. What he needed was someone like me with star quality.

Within a coupla days, I posed for lots of pictures. Mostly in Clift's apartment. Clothes on, clothes off. He had me study pictures of Marilyn Monroe and then pretend to be sexy like her. Since he was a professional photographer, Clift collected oodles of photos—mostly of dead movie stars. Even had one of Auntie Em. And lotsa Dorothy. James Dean, too.

After a few days, Clift hypnotized me. That's when he discovered I was Elvis in my former life. Under hypnosis, I told Clift things about Elvis that no one knew before. Stuff about him bein' gay. Started in the army before he met Priscilla and lasted until the day he died. He always had a bodyguard who was his secret boyfriend. While in a trance, I explained to Clift how Elvis got infected with AIDS; not from sex but from shootin' up all them drugs he took.

When I woke up, I'd never remember anything; Clift would kindly remind me.

He was good to me. He got some 8 x 10 glossies made of me and sent them to casting agents. He liked to say he was my Colonel Parker. And he was.

I got some meetings with these agents—at their houses in the Hollywood Hills. Clift said it would be a good idea to do whatever they wanted, so I did. Most of 'em just wanted to stare at me. Or take Polaroid pictures for their files. One really rich one insisted on cutting off some of my pubic hair and puttin' it in a box with the pubic hairs of other young boys who became famous actors. Like John Travolta and that Leonardo with the name I can't pronounce, he said.

I never did no tryouts—even though I was willin' to perform my version of "You Ain't Nothing But a Hound Dog." I sometimes left with a wada money, though, which helped pay for me and Clift to survive.

By this time, we were lovers, like Elvis and his bodyguard. Sex with guys came pretty natural to me—probably 'cause I was Elvis reborn and he hadn't worked out all his homosexualness in his last life. According to Clift, sex and death was married. And since Elvis and I have the same soul, I was born with AIDS. I just needed to become a star before I died—like that River Phoenix did.

Clift started gettin' real sick right before Christmas. I took pretty good care of him—like I had taken care of my poor Mama. When he stopped arrangin' appointments with casting agents, I'd go out on the streets and make some cash.

You shoulda seen the expression on some of those guys' faces when I told 'em my name was Elvis. They'd look at me like I was a Science Fair Project.

Clift and I celebrated my first Christmas in Hollywood together. He had this little fake silver tree and ornaments he'd made hisself with pictures of dead stars on 'em. There was Judy and Marilyn and all those ones from *Rebel Without a Cause*. He put an angel ornament on top of the tree: a picture of the real Elvis.

The day after Christmas, I came home from makin' some money and found Clift. He was layin' on the couch—wearin' his long black cape and lotsa black eye makeup. Dead as all them movie stars hangin' on the glittery tree. He'd put a plastic bag over his head. He left me a note, sayin' how we'd meet again in another life: like the Colonel and Elvis would.

I got thrown outta the Suicide Hotel. Now I'm livin' on the streets. No home to go to. No Mama. No Auntie Em. I'm not sure if I'll ever be a movie star.

I've lost a lotta weight—so much it's become a joke when I tell people my name is Elvis. Nobody wants me anymore. Or thinks I'm very special.

I miss Clift. No matter what, he loved me. Insteada fame and money, Elvis got loved in his lifetime. Real love—even if it was homolove. Pretty great, don'tcha think?

After Beckett and Before Elvis

C. B. McCLINTOCK

When I met Joel Pumpkin, I never in a million years would have guessed he was a boring man. A fantastically boring man. When I met Joel Pumpkin, he was eating a cucumber sandwich with Gorgonzola cheese, mustard, and mayonnaise on Irish brown bread, drinking mulled cider, wearing a pince-nez, and reading *Ulysses.* I was in love.

Until I found out that I had only met him while he was in his Joyce stage, one of the better ones we've endured. Whenever he asked me to do something and I agreed to, I had to reply, "yes I said yes I will yes" ("Honey, will you make spaghetti tonight?" "Yes I said yes I will yes"); he took French classes and subjected me to the same; and we spent every Sunday searching for a blind street named North Richmond.

We never did find it, because the Gertrude Stein stage followed close on the heels of the Joyce stage, during which Joel wore nothing but brown corduroy suits, started collecting Picasso posters (all our budget would allow), and made such pronouncements as "Breakfast is east." When he started trying to write *my* autobiography I told him to lose the Stein phase or lose me.

After Stein came Bowles (he turned the thermostat up to 85 degrees and wallpapered the entire place in a desert motif); after Bowles came Bukowski (one of the worst ever— we spent most of our time hanging around post offices or drinking ourselves blind); after Bukowski came O'Connor (Flannery, that is, and one of our most pleasant stretches— visiting peacocks and looking for Red Sammy's Famous Bar- becue —until Joel started bringing home prosthetic limbs for me to try on); and after O'Connor came The Last Straw and The Last Straw was named Beckett and the Beckett phase went a little something like this:

"Can I bury you in sand?"

"No."

"Just up to your waist?"

"No."

"How about you just sit in an empty trash can?"

"No."

"But I'll be in one, too."

"No."

"For me?"

"No."

So he sat in his trash can alone and mumbled to the wall; when we ate dinner together and I asked him to pass the salt he'd say, "I can't reach the salt. (*Pause*) I will reach the salt. (*Pause*) I must reach the salt" before he'd even move a muscle; and when he started miming is when I delivered The Ultimatum to The Last Straw: take on the personality of someone I like or I leave.

For weeks Joel Pumpkin was no one. After Beckett and before Elvis I found out just who Joel Pumpkin was on his own: he was no one. He was the type of man who would eat egg salad sandwiches—made with low-fat mayonnaise and no pepper—on white bread for every meal for the rest of his life unless you stepped in and stopped him. Without someone to become, Joel Pumpkin was the type of man who would wear clothes made entirely of blue terry cloth every day for the rest of his life unless you stepped in and stopped him. Joel Pumpkin was himself for three weeks. I kept a bag of my belongings at work at all times.

Then came the glorious day when I opened the door to our apartment and smelled something frying. The entire place was hung heavy with that unmistakable smell: the buttery, somewhat coppery, cholesterol-y smell of something frying. And that is when Joel appeared in the doorway of the kitchen. So began the greatest day of my life.

He had become Elvis. Unmistakably Elvis. Everything about him was Elvis: the way he stood, his right shoulder held slightly back, his left shoulder slightly forward, his black shoes shining and his feet apart, positioned as his shoulders were (right foot forward, left foot back); his whole stance suggesting he was about to race off into something fiery and important. His hair was parted on the right and crested down onto his forehead like a wave; his pants were black and his jacket was black and his shirt was white and slightly open at the collar and as he stood like that in the doorway I first heard the long, slow, succulent Southern syllables he spoke: "Would you like a fried peanut butter–and-banana sandwich, ma'am?"

"Yes," I said. "Please."

Joel had never gone this far before. He had never taken on the actual *voice* of anyone before—he might have learned the language they spoke, but he didn't affect a chirpy brogue when he became Joyce; he didn't slur every gravelly sentence when he was Bukowski. And this time he dyed his blond hair black. For good. And this time I've stopped calling him Joel. For good.

I take rolls and rolls of pictures of him: I pose Elvis on the couch and throw piles of letters on his lap and at his feet, as if they were fan mail; I sit him at a piano in a music store and tell him to pout; I perch him on a diner stool and have him look sidelong at me, one eyebrow cocked, past empty seats and dishes. When I look through that lens I realize that Elvis is like Orson Welles: when each was young, he had the most memorable voice of his time and was the most beautiful man of his time. In my pictures, Elvis is young again. In my life, Elvis is young again. In my life, Elvis is alive. And Elvis is mine.

Elvis' Rabbi

MURRAY HORWITZ

Lights up on Rabbi, an elderly white man.

RABBI: We walked, we talked. We talked of . . . many things. Torah, Talmud. He was very interested in what constitutes a moral life, an ethical life. I says, "Look—it's always a struggle. The important thing is to study, to work, to do."

He was very interested in the whole concept of *teshuvah,* of changing. I remember before one Yom Kippur he was reading Agnon's *The Days of Awe.* He was fascinated by the idea of *teshuvah,* that a man could change, could turn back to G-d—that he *must* do it. He felt this to be a moral imperative. I says, "Look—look at your own work." After all, any artistic decision has moral consequences. And you can see it in his career—although he felt he was an absolute failure at this—always the return to his heritage, to his people. His service in the military. The decision to stop making pictures. The television special. There was always this fear he confessed to me of letting go, of disappointing his fans, of not staying on the same path—and yet all the time this burning need he felt to change, to turn back, to really *do teshuvah.*

He was constantly struggling with the demands of *halachah*—should he keep kosher, should he not . . . I says, "Look—you'll do what you can do. So every once in a while, you won't eat the sausage." I says, "You know what's good? A little peanut butter and banana. Wonderful!" Who knew?

Had a fine sense of history. He was all the time worried about his place in it. Not so much how he would be remembered; more about whether he was an agent of progress, of transformative social change. This troubled him. All the time he says to me, "Rabbi—think about it: all the people who really changed the course of Western civilization were Jews: Christ, Marx, Freud." Then he says, "Manny Gelernter!" I says, "Who?" He says, "Manny Gelernter—he makes a cabbage soup, could *really* change your life." (*Pause*) Had an excellent sense of humor.

We talked, we talked. (*Pause*) Used to ask me a lot about an afterlife. I says, "Who knows?" I says, "Look—"

Blackout.

Eddie James "Son" House Jr. (1902–1988)

ERIC G. CHALEK

Detroit, Michigan, 1981

So you wan know bout tha Blues.
Now, you bin lisnin them rock-roll
recuds, wondern where they git dat
sou-ound. Bin lisnin'a Elvis
Presly, wondern bout where he come
from. He come out tha blues sound.
Tha blues. But, see, blues is a
feelin. A low-down feelin.
You cin git tha blues bout yo'
fella man, or wumin.
Or you cin git tha blues,
if yo're really unlucky,
you cin git tha blues bout Gawd
an'a Devul. Now whin
most peoples whin they think
a tha blues, think:
"My wumin done me wrong,
I'ma gonna go 'n jump
from tha bridge!" 'At's ole Elvis'
blues. But that ain't what
ree-al blues is. Ree-al blues
ain't bout no Heartbreakin Hotel.
                    Ree-al blues
come from tha woids 'n tha voises
an'a meanins of a song.

Now, one guy, he staht out
a song wid "Lawd ha' moicy
on me, whin I die."
Now I don' wan dat, don'
wan dat. I wan some'a
that moicy now! Tha blues,
see, sits on yo' head. Now you
staht out an' you don' feel
so bad, but affa while
it give you a headache,
then you cain't sleep no mohr
cause it won' git off
yo' head. Then you cain't see
straight, cause it makin you,
makin you go bli-ind.
See.
Thas whin you got tha blues.
                    Now whin you got tha blues
bout somebody, 'at's easist blues
ta have: 'at's dem rock-roll
blues 'at eva-one's singin.
You ain't gonna keell
yoself bout no wumin. Keellin
someboda else, 'at's easy. Havin
tha blues bout yo' fella man or
wumin's easy, cause people
is people 'n they git somethin
from Gawd fer doin you wrong.
Now, havin tha blues bout Gawd,
now dat's not so easy.
                    Gawd an'a Devul don' woik so good tagetha,
                    'at's their
problem. Trouble is it's yo' problem
too. Now ere's some guys,
I use ta know said, "I traded
my soul ta tha Devul so I

cin play tha best blues you eva hoird!"
And they was proud of it. An' they
some meeen blues. But
they was stupid, 's what they were.
I done nuff preachin, read u-nuff
scripchu ta know that dealin
with tha Devul ain't gonna make Gawd
real happy. See Gawd
an'a Devul don' much care fo' eachudder.
        Now, sometimes tha Devul come round sayin,
        "Son,
why you so misabul? I make
you feel betta, git you happy
home, git you ridda them blues.
You jis-uh put down-nat bottul,
and lisin'a me." An' I tell him
I don' wan none 'a his. I'll stick
ta my bottul, cause tha bottul
and tha blues is betta fo' tha soul
than ainithin ole Lucifer
cin gimmie. I's drinkin
'at ole Meducin since nineteen
an' twenti-sevin, but I neva
took nuthin from tha Devul. Evuh. See,
Gawd ratha me be drunk'asa skunk
'an be in co-hoots wi-tha Devul.
Now, I ain't tawlk'd it ovuh
wit Gawd, but he don' do much
tawkin. Leest none 'at I cin hee-uh.
But I figures 'at I'm right
bout tha bottul. Betta ta be
ina bottul, than a' be trapped
in Hay-ull. Tha Devul, he love
ta tawlk, but Gawd gots nuff ta do
thana tawlk wit ole Son.
So I grab me a bottul an'a gi-tar,

and I tawk ta Gawd my own way.
                    Now,
I us'a preach lots. I wudn't what you cawl an eye-tinut
preachuh, but I moved from town 'na town
preachin', didn't have no choich though,
I's jus spreadin tha Woid on Sundays and singin
tha blues on tha week. So on Monay,
Tuesay, Wesday, so on, I's drinkin and playin
tha blues, but on Sunday mownin, I's playin
differnt tunes—wit tha same woids. Now, you cin
do dat wit tha blues. Ya jis stick
tha woids "Gawd help me, please" in front, and "A—men"
at tha end, an' you got whut they cawls
a spee-i-chal. 'S'all da same.
That's why its tha blues.
                    Now whin you got blues bout Gawd
an'a' Devul,
you got blues bout makin yo' mind fo' one
or tha otha. Tha scripchus tell us act
once, but think twi-ice—See—cause tha Devul
beat Gawd ta yo' mouth nine times outa te-in.
Jees-us is comin fo' tha quick an'a dead, well
you damn we-ull don' wanna be tha quick.
So I al-ways folla my se-cund
mind. Nevuh tha foist mind; Cause 'at,
'at's tha Devul's mind.
                    Now you kids come up hee-ah, lookin
fa' me ta tell you bout
tha blues, and now
you got it.
See, you kids these days,
thinkin that tha blues is
bout wimmins 'n' drinkin,
'n'a postman,
'n'a houn'og,
'n'a jay-all,

141

'n'a all dat silluniss;
but now
dat you hoid me tawkin
bout Gawd, an' you bin thinkin
bout Gawd, an' you ree-lize
bout Gawd—you got tha blues.
Cause now you caught between
Gawd and tha Devul
jes like me.
'Ats tha Blues.
'Ats tha ree-al Blues.

Heartburn Hotel

CLIFFORD R. MURPHY

James, a twentysomething New Hampshire Yankee. The kind of a guy you have trouble taking seriously. Talks in a rambling, mock-Southern preacher style.

JAMES: It was 1996, on the 61st birthday of Elvis Aron Presley, and plunged in the depths of our extreme northern ignorance of the culinary arts of Gladys Love Presley, my friend Buck Tulas and I ventured to make some fried peanut butter–and-nanner sandwiches, in honor of the King. Now, I know they're *fried*, but I *thought* they were supposed to be *deep* fried. So there we stood—big nanner-eatin' grins on our faces, and canola oil running down our chins the whole time. It did me in. Buck was fine, but I couldn't go to work for a week. Triggered some sort of deep-down sick, the kind of sick you hear about on PBS. Anyway, I couldn't go to the bathroom, I couldn't eat, I couldn't go to work. It seemed the world was coming to some sort of grease-induced end. The only real piece of mind I could find was in "Poke Salad Annie" from "Elvis: Live on Stage." It was the vision of all that roughage dancing in my head. Somehow it seemed more heavenly than "How Great Thou Art." Even still, I suffered.

Then one day it hit me, like a flash. It wasn't the grease making me sick. Sure, I had gorged. Sure, I had suffered. I had eaten sausage spoon bread and black-eyed peas and gravy. I'd had seventeen glazed donuts and one apple fritter over the course of Elvis' birthday week, but it had *nothing to do with that*. It *wasn't* the food. It was that I hadn't *finished*. I'd left out the most essential element, the yang to the yin of dining.

Dessert.

Sure enough, I settled myself into bed, and started to feed. Later on that night my fever, and several unmentionables, passed. Took care of business in a flash. My digestive virtue lay broken like so many cherry stems and whipped cream cans of The Great 20-Hot-Fudge-Sundae Massacre. After a week of suffering in the name of The King, I had found my rest in the Sabbath of dairy. The ice cream sundae.

Sister Blues

ELENA CARRILLO

Alice and The Fat Elvis (an obese Elvis impersonator, only seen in silhouette). Empty stage. Alice is in a spotlight in front of a scrim. There is a covered birthday cake next to her. We hear Elvis singing the tail end of "Blue Suede Shoes."

ALICE: August 16, 1977. Elvis Presley dropped dead. (*Beat*) I was glad he ate himself to death! I was only sorry he had to do it on my birthday!

My sister Edith, she's older than me by a decade. We never did get along. She said I killed him.

She was a major Elvis geek! That's all she cared about! All her stupid albums and all that bric-a-brac crap, kitchen magnets and posters! And I especially hated that wacky head-bobber thing! It made Elvis look like an advertisement for Colgate!

"Alice! That's an antique!" Edith would say. Junk is junk! I say. Then she would try to throw me out of her room. But it was my room too, so I always came back.

I didn't ask for him to die on my birthday. What did I know? I was only six! Besides I had already apologized seven hundred and fifty billion times for breaking her stupid Elvis lamp! Edith thought I was a pest. (*Pause*)

Our dad met Elvis in the army. Dad wasn't impressed. He'd say, "all them screaming gals, trying to get a touch of him when he passed. . . ."

"What was he was like, Dad?" Edith would beg.

"They put his scrawny ass on the scale and shaved all that hair off. . . ."

I liked the thought of Elvis completely bald.

"As white and soft as a hard-boiled egg," Dad used to describe it. "Same as anybody else's bald head. . . ."

But Edith thought that was just "Far out." Appalling. My sister was a fanatic.

When I was twelve, my sister broke up with her boyfriend and rather than waste the money on the tickets she had bought for them to go to Memphis on the anniversary of Elvis' death, she decided to drag me to Graceland with her. There she is, dragging me from site to site, "Look at this, Alice, look at this!" Clicking snapshots with her camera all the way. Click click. Click click. I just wanted to go home. And Edith was like, "Alice, you're so inconsiderate!"

She wanted *me* to be considerate! Didn't she ever just once think that maybe I would have rather been doing something, *any*thing else on my birthday?

"I don't know why you have to be so impatient," she would say, clicking away. "It's not like we get to come to the home of Elvis every year. This is a historical event!"

Disneyland! Fantasyland! I don't know . . . Iceland! That's something to get excited about! But Graceland? Do you have any idea what it's like in Memphis in August? I had sweat running down my legs, and the mob was incredible. People shoving, elbows in my face, fat ladies with beehive hairdos, men with pompadours, people clutching at souvenirs like religious relics. (*Imitating her sister with a pantomime camera: snap snap snap*) "Isn't it wonderful? It's just too unreal!"

Unreal was right. By the end of the day I was nauseous from watching good, bad, and indifferent Elvis impersonators in the lounge of our hotel. They were having a competition. The audience was supposed to vote for a winner. So there's this whole slew of Elvises, all gyrating their hips and belting out old faves: "Blue Hawaii," "Blue Moon of Kentucky," and "Milkcow Blues Boogie."

And *my* sister, boy, she was hanging like a salami over the back of her seat. (*Clapping, pointing, trying to pick her winner*) "That one! Much better! No, *that* one! *That* one!"

I was already in the pissiest mood imaginable. Dinner had been some sort of nightmare Elvis special with chicken-fried steak and green peas and mashed potatoes and gravy and corn on the cob and it was basically an all-you-can-eat-deal, though I couldn't even manage the first serving.

To make the event a complete nausea-inducing experi-ence, Edith had the chef bring out a special birthday cake for dessert. It was *so* thoughtful. A cake in the shape of a guitar. It said "The King Lives" across the frets in blue icing. How nice. (*Takes a pretend photograph, smiling plastically*) "Smile, Alice, this will make such a great picture: You and your cake."

As Alice talks, The Fat Elvis in silhouette enters and moves toward an enormous spotlight illuminating center stage like a full moon. Dead center, the silhouette of a microphone awaits.

I thought the whole night was going to be a complete and tragic washout when all of the sudden, this big fat Arab—a guy way too fat for the King even, if you can believe it—came lumbering out onto the floor in the Vegas-look with rings on his fingers and glimmer from his head to his toes. He didn't look a thing like Elvis, and I almost laughed myself out of my seat.

This guy was totally slobbulous! As he waddled across the stage, his stomach jiggled, his cheeks jiggled, his glitter jig-gled. This guy worked up a sweat just getting to the micro-phone!

My sister was embarrassed and appalled. Partly by my braying like a mule, and partly by the sight of the gross mass of Elvis zealotry whipping back his hair and preparing to compete against at least a dozen other better-looking, look-alikes who had gone before him.

And *then*, this guy started to sing.

The stage washes blue. Elvis' rendition of "Blue Moon" from Sun Sessions *is heard. It is eerie. Alice stares, transfixed.*

I stopped laughing. This guy could not only sing, but he was incredible. He *was* the voice of Elvis!

The Fat Elvis "sings" his heart out.

When it came time to vote, Edith went for the slick, Early-Elvis look of a New Yorker named Jerry Campodifiori. He was good. He sang "Jailhouse Rock" and had the leg shift and the pelvis-thing going pretty good. He even sang okay, I guess. (*Pause*)

I voted for Abud.

"You're just doing that to be spiteful!" Edie screamed at me. "You don't care who wins!"

She wanted me to vote for Jerry. She thought I was just being mean. Making fun of her. But I was voting in earnest. I really thought he should have won.

The Fat Elvis is keening in the background.

Jerry didn't win either. Edith was mad at me for the rest of the night. And after that trip she went away to college.

God, I was never so happy! No more birthdays with Elvis cakes or any more accusations about killing him. "Won't you just be *so* happy?" Edith said acidly.

I wasn't *so* happy. Edith leaving didn't stop the networks from airing Elvis memorials and marathons and sing-alongs. Year after year. I had my room all to myself and the phone all to myself and the record player all to myself. Sometimes I would think about Memphis, and that fat Arab and I would get lonely.

Spotlight on The Fat Elvis fades to black.

When Edith came back, she had put away all her Elvis records and posters and her head-bobber thingie. I said, "Hey Edie, I killed Elvis." She said, "Yeah. Whatever." I said, "Hey

Edie, Elvis is a twit." She said, "Right, uh-huh." I didn't get it! I said, "Hey Edie, for my birthday I hope you're not planning on hogging the TV to watch all those stupid follow-the-bouncing-ball sing-alongs on cable." She said, "I'm busy." (*Pause*)

On my birthday I watched *Blue Hawaii* by myself. I realized that Edith had stopped doing her hair like Ann-Margret.

Alice picks up the cake at her side, lights the single candle on it.

On my birthday, she baked me a cake. A regular two-layer round with the kind of filling I liked. It had blue roses on it.

"What? No guitars?" I said. "No 'Viva Las Vegas'? No hound dogs or 'Elvis-killer'?"

She reads the cake.

Happy Birthday Alice. Then Edith pointed out the trellis of frosting on the side and the words she had scrawled in icing there: P. S. Don't mess with my blue suede shoes.

Alice laughs. Spotlight fades slowly to black. Alice smiles in the warm glow of the candlelight.

Long live the King.

Alice blows out the candle. Blackout.

Elvis: Before/After

Brad Bailey knew his entertainment career was about to hit bottom, his 305-pound body pulling him down as surely as a lead anchor.

He could feel it as he spun his body, as he gyrated his hips, as his chest heaved with each breath that shaped the lyrics to Elvis Presley's "Suspicious Minds."

There he was—as if in a dream—on the stage in the crowded night club north of Phoenix. He looked, he sounded like his idol at the moment the King of Rock 'n' Roll died, an obese hulk at the age of 42.

But this Elvis impersonator was only 28. Shy and retiring offstage, he was a bachelor afraid to ask a girl out on a date.

Days, he earned a decent living running his own business. Nights, for the pure joy of it, he would re-create the magic and excitement of Elvis. "I felt more comfortable portraying him than being myself," Brad admits today.

Brad remembers his first performance singing "Blue Suede Shoes." "The applause hooked me right away." But once off the platform, out of the glare of the spotlight, he had trouble connecting with his admiring public. "I was too timid to look people in the eye," he recalls.

Moderately overweight as a youth, Brad started to put on excess pounds when he was sidelined from playing baseball two years ago with a knee injury. "Being single, it was easy to make a steady diet out of cheeseburgers, french fries, and soft drinks." Card games with friends featured pizza smothered with sausage, Canadian bacon, and extra cheese. "I could wolf down seven or eight pieces real quick," he recalls.

With his body straining to carry his weight, Brad was too winded to play softball, the sport that helped him burn calories. He had trouble breathing when he slept. His size 44 jeans were so tight circulation was almost cut off. Yet pride kept him from buying specially tailored clothes.

Brad wanted to date but was too embarrassed to even ask. "I knew that if I wasn't attractive, how would an attractive girl want to go out with me? I had no self-confidence and I wouldn't even try," he says. "There were times I just wanted to call it quits . . . I mean life."

Then came the night a year ago in that club near Phoenix, the night that became Brad Bailey's personal watershed, his turning point.

As always, he was doing his thing. But this time, it was harder to make the turns, to do the splits, even breathe. His face was drenched with perspiration, and suddenly Brad Bailey was taken with the notion that he would die that night like his idol.

"At that moment I realized something had to be done," Brad recalls. "Otherwise, I would never make it to my 42nd birthday. I didn't want to leave this world looking like Elvis."

Encouraged by a disc-jockey friend at a local radio station who had lost weight and kept it off, Brad tried something revolutionary that week a year ago. It was not another failed diet but a weight loss plan that's been working for millions for nearly twenty years.

Brad walked into his nearby weight loss center. "I was determined. If this didn't work for me, there'd be nothing left," he remembers.

"The difference I found there," he says, "is that I never got hungry and the food wasn't cardboard. It was delicious. For a bachelor used to junk food, it was perfect." Each meal was prepared in convenient calorie- and portion-controlled servings. There were three nutritionally balanced meals, as well as three snacks each day.

Brad loved the Ravioli, Lasagna, and Spaghetti with Meatballs. He was able to choose from a smorgasbord of tempting entrees such as Barbecue Beef, Spicy Oriental Chicken, and Beef Enchiladas. Even his favorite—Thick Crust Extra Cheesy Pizza. For desserts Brad feasted on Fudge Cupcakes, Vanilla and Chocolate Pudding, and Caramel Popcorn. "I couldn't believe I could eat all that delicious food and still lose weight," he laughs.

"The pounds just vanished," says Brad. "The first week on the program I lost seven pounds. It felt great. The next week I lost six. Then I started to feel my pants getting real loose. I knew I was on my way."

As he continued to shed more and more weight, Brad also gained insight into how to make his losses permanent. He learned a whole battery of weight maintenance strategies: chewing slowly, making an occasion out of each meal, and other easy-to-do attitudes to eating.

In all, Brad lost 100 pounds, nose-diving from a 44- to a 34-inch waist. 6 foot 1 inch, Brad Bailey weighs 205 today. He sees a girl now. And he's back playing baseball.

Onstage, Brad has retired the huge jumpsuit used for his Elvis impressions. What the audience sees is a younger, leaner version of the Legend of Rock. "The splits come easy now," smiles Brad Bailey, as he sizzles in the role of the man in the Blue Suede Shoes.

Contributors

SHELLEY BERC is a playwright and novelist. Her plays include *A Girl's Guide to the Divine Comedy, Dial Heads, Burn Out, Shooting Shiva,* and *Stations. Rameau's Nephew,* based on Diderot, cowritten with Andre Belgrader, was performed in 1990 at CSC Rep, which also premiered their version of *Scapin.* The American Repertory Theatre has produced the Berc/Belgrader adaptation of *Servant of Two Masters* and commissioned their musical, *Ubu Rock.* Berc's work has been performed at CSC, Yale Rep, ACT, and ART, and in theatre festivals throughout Europe. *A Girl's Guide to the Divine Comedy* was recently published in *Plays for the End of the Century.* Her novel, *The Shape of Wilderness,* was published by Coffee House Press.

JAN BUTTRAM is a recipient of the Roger L. Stevens award from the Kennedy Center's Fund for New American Plays and has received a major grant from the Berrilla Kerr Foundation. Her plays have been produced off-Broadway, off-off Broadway, and regionally. Her word is published by Samuel French and Smith and Kraus. Buttram is the artistic director of Abingdon Theatre Company in New York, and as an actress she has played regionally and off-Broadway, and has toured nationally.

ELENA CARRILLO has had play readings and productions at the University of Texas at El Paso, as a winning finalist of the 1996 Border PlayFest at the Border Book Festival in Las Cruces, New Mexico, and as a winning finalist at the Word-BRIDGE Playwrights Lab in St. Petersburg, Florida. She is also the assistant editor of *The Students' Guide to Playwriting Opportunities* and the recipient of the 1995 Oscar G. Brockett Award in Theatre History. Her play *Call the Serpent God to Me* received an honorable mention at the 1996 Twenty-first Century Playwrights Festival in New York.

ERIC G. CHALEK wishes that he played slide guitar—or any instrument, for that matter. In fact, other than brief flirtations with piano, trombone, and harmonica, he has only been able to make music by turning on the radio. And even then, he usually gets static. He recently graduated from Gettysburg College and hopes that a career is in his future.

CYNTHIA L. COOPER's plays have been produced in a variety of venues in New York, across the U. S., and Canada. *How She Played the Game* was produced off-Broadway by The Women's Project and Productions, had an off-Broadway reprise at Primary Stages, has been performed in theatres in fifty location including Reno, Boston, Michigan, Vancouver, Pennsylvania, New Jersey, and on Lifetime TV, and is included in four anthologies, among them *Women Heroes* (Applause). *Sisters of Sisters*, winner of the Hutchinson Festival of New Plays, was produced in Kansas, Minnesota, and in New York at the American Renaissance Theatre; *Slow Burn* was produced in New York by Wings Theatre; *Strange Bedfellows* was produced by The Women's Theatre Project in Minnesota and presented at West Coast Playwrights; *Fox and Hounds* was winner in the Double Image Festival of Short Plays and won two other short play awards; and *The World at Your Fingertips* (coauthor), a musical for young people, was performed in New York and toured in twenty states. Other plays include *Twenty-Four Hours in the Life of the Belted Sandfish*, *Mountain* (one-act), *Dirty Laundry*, and *Beyond Stone*. A playwright-in-residence at the Playwrights' Center in Minneapolis for two years, she directed the Women's Playwriting Conference there. She had two selections included in Heinemann's *Baseball Monologues*. Working as a freelance author in New York, she has five nonfiction books to her credit, including *Mockery of Justice: The True Story of the Sheppard Murder*

Case, which was featured on NBC *Dateline* and will air as a CBS TV movie.

TAD CURRY was born in Evanston, Illinois, went to school in Pennsylvania, and now lives in New Hampshire. He spends his winters working in order to have fun during his summers. That fun usually focuses around long-distance hiking or cycling, but he has been known to hang around summer theatres, making himself useful. He is the worst actor in his family. He is single and would love to meet Lisa-Marie. This is his first publication.

GAY DAVIDSON-ZIELSKE lives in Madison and works teaching composition, literature, creative writing, and screenwriting at the University of Wisconsin–Whitewater. Her recent work can be found in *Baseball Monologues* (Heinemann), *For She Is the Tree of Life* (Conari Press), and *Detours: Travel by Land, Air, Sea, and Mind* (Lonesome Traveller Cooperative Press, Madison). She coedited *Straight from the Heart*, an anthology of love poetry for Lonesome Traveller, and is sole editor of *Detours*. Her time is poorly distributed among mothering, writing, daydreaming, and driving, driving, driving.

KAREN DE WITT, a longtime journalist, has worked for the *Pittsburgh Courier, New York Post, USA Today, Washington Post*, and is currently a reporter in the Washington Bureau of the *New York Times*. Her free-lance articles have appeared in numerous publications, including *Glamour, Essence, Washingtonian*, and *National Geographic*. Widely traveled, she makes her home in Washington, D.C.

BILL EVANS was born in Forty Fort, Pennsylvania, and has lived in New York City for the past twenty years. His poems have appeared in a wide variety of publications, and he is a frequent and accomplished performer of his own work. He is also the author of two full-length plays for children, *Amazon A-Go-Go* and *Fortune's Friends*, both performed in Manhattan.

STEVE FEFFER's plays include *The Wizards of Quiz, Marilyn & Marc, The Mystery Catcher, Mr. Rebbetzin,* and *Bart, the Temp, A Story of Wall Street: A Contemporary Stage Version of Melville's Bartleby.* His work has been produced or developed by theatres that include the O'Neill National Playwrights Conference, Ensemble Studio Theatre, Philadelphia Festival Theatre for New Plays, National Jewish Theatre, Nantucket Short Play Festival, and the Victory Gardens Theatre. *The Wizards of Quiz* is published by Dramatists Play Service. Two of his theatre pieces on the national pastime appear in Heinemann's *Baseball Monologues.* He is a recipient of a New Plays Grant from the Council of Jewish Theatres and the Jewish Endowment for the Humanities. Steve has a BFA in Dramatic Writing from New York University and an MFA in Playwriting from the University of Iowa Playwrights Workshop. He has taught playwriting at Young Playwrights Inc., NYC; the Playwrights Theatre of New Jersey; Middlesex Arts High School for Talented and Gifted Students; Rutgers University's Art Matters Too!; and the University of Iowa; and writing and literature at New York University, Iona College, and Centenary College. Steve would like to thank Elvis, alive and well and working at a local kosher butcher's shop, for his great assistance in preparing this monologue.

CRAIG FOLS is an actor/playwright whose first play, *Buck Simple,* opened the 1994–1995 season at LaMama E.T.C. Club and was subsequently published in Applause's anthology *The Best American Short Plays of 1994–1995.* Other plays have been presented at the Williamstown Theatre Festival and the Currican Theatre, New York. He is a 1995 recipient of the Berrilla Kerr Award in Playwriting.

TERRY GALLOWAY is a playwright, poet, essayist, and performer. She holds a degree in American Studies from the University of Texas, Austin. She has published a play, a performance text, a book of poetry, and many monologues and articles. She cowrote an award-winning PBS children's show. She lives in the part of Florida that is not Miami Beach.

JUDY GEBAUER's plays include *Reclaimed* (Long Wharf Theatre; recipient of the Steinberg Playwriting Award for Excellence; finalist for the Susan Smith Blackburn Award); *Bobby Sands, M.P.* (Philadelphia Festival Theatre; Irish Arts Center; winner of the HBO Writers Award and the Dennis McIntyre Playwriting Award); and *The Hidden Ones* (Philadelphia Festival Theatre; winner of the W. Alton Jones Foundation Grant). Her play *A Ceremony Without Crystal* received Grand Prize in the 1996 Colorado Women Playwrights Project. Her one-act *The Nip and the Bite* is published in the anthology *Facing Forward* (Broadway Play Publishing) and . . . *a catcher to his pitcher* appears in *Baseball Monologues* (Heinemann). Her novel *Sawyer's Man* was a finalist in the Bantam/20th Century Fox-First Western Competition. Her play *The Fire-Bringer* was commissioned by the Denver Center Theatre Company. GeBauer is an Associate in the Rocky Mountain Women's Institute and a recipient of the Colorado Federation of the Arts Innovation Award. Her new plays are *Trancas* and *American Dogwood*.

DAVID AND CAROL HEGBERG. This is Dave's first attempt at professional writing. He started the story, then Carol finished it. Dave is a postal carrier while Carol is a homemaker/writer. Her last published piece was a script, *Secret of the Gifts*, for Meriwether Publishing of Colorado Springs. The Hegbergs have been married 27 years, have three children, and have never had a fight. They reside in DeKalb, Illinois.

FRANK HIGGINS is the author of *The Sweet By n' By*, published by Dramatists Play Service, which starred Blythe Danner and Gwyneth Paltrow. His new play, *Miracles*, deals with a teenaged autistic savant and her charismatic teacher. He lives in Kansas City, Missouri.

RICHARD HOLODY is an assistant professor of social work at Lehman College, Bronx, New York, and author of two full-length plays, *Chorizos Tacos*, which recently had a reading on

Theatre Row, and *Heather's Babies*. Both plays focus on the problems of social workers and their clients in the inner city.

MURRAY HORWITZ is the coauthor of *Ain't Misbehavin'* (winner of the 1978 Tony and New York Drama Critics Circle awards for Best Musical) and *Haarlem Nocturne* (LaMama & Broadway, 1984; Crossroads Theatre, 1995). He is the coauthor, with Wynton Marsalis, of the 1996 National Public Radio series *Making the Music* (Peabody Award), and is the Vice President of Cultural Programming at NPR. A graduate of Kenyon College in Ohio, he lives with his wife and three children in Maryland, where he received a 1997 Governor's Arts Award for playwriting.

MARGARET HUNT has written eight full-length plays, including *Down at Johnnie D's*, which was produced in 1995 on Theatre Row in New York City. She has also written a number of short plays, including *Bread, Blue Lips and Fingertips,* and *Fire Flies*. She is a recipient of a 1994 Playwright's Fellowship from the Berrilla Kerr Foundation and two Playwright's Residencies from the Edward Albee Foundation. She is a member of The Women's Project and Productions, Circle Rep Playwrights Lab, the BMI Librettists Workshop, and the Dramatists Guild.

MICHAEL KEARNS is an internationally acclaimed solo performer. His solo work includes *The Truth Is Bad Enough, intimacies, more intimacies, Rock,* and *Attachments*. He is the author of *T-Cells & Sympathy, Acting = Life,* and *Getting Your Solo Act Together*. He lives in Los Angeles.

TIM J. LORD is currently a student at Knox College in Galesburg, Illinois, studying theatre and English literature. He has had a one-act play, *Springes to Catch Woodcocks*, published in *Catch*, Knox's literary magazine, and is working on another one-act, *Bridge Over the River Khan*, as well as an as-yet-untitled full-length. He hopes to pursue an MFA in playwriting after graduation and would like to thank Stuart Sharpe who served as "Elvis Expert," supplying the playwright with information that inspired "Calling Elvis."

CARA B. MCCLINTOCK has a degree in literature from Gettysburg College and shares her birthdate with Elvis himself. [So does Michael Kearns.—*Ed.*] She recently moved from Pennsylvania to Massachusetts, where she can be found drinking pots of coffee and working on several essays and short stories. Many of her favorite authors are mentioned in her monologue printed here; among those omitted are W. B. Yeats and Harriet Doerr. Ms. McClintock would like to dedicate this monologue to her family and to Peter Walsh.

MAUREEN MCCOY is the author of three novels, *Walking After Midnight, Summertime,* and *Divining Blood,* all published by Poseidon/Simon & Schuster. She has published stories and Irish-travel articles. Her other published "Elvis-inspired" writing includes the novel *Walking After Midnight* and the short story "The Sugarees." She has recently lived in Galway, Ireland, and been in residence at Hawthornden Castle, the international retreat for writers, and the Helene Wurlitzer Foundation of Taos, New Mexico, where she worked on Elvis monologues and a new novel. Maureen McCoy teaches at Cornell University.

JAMES R. MILLER was born in Salt Lake City, raised in the Midwest, and began writing and acting solo pieces for competition and for local Illinois community theatres while still in high school. After he spent four years in the Marine Corps as both a combat journalist and a satellite specialist, he began publishing work in newspapers and international magazines. His monologue, *A Changing Season,* appears in *Baseball Monologues* (Heinemann). Twenty-five years old, he resides in DeKalb, Illinois, where he owns a successful fitness business. He is currently finishing his first full-length novel and working on a book of poetry.

LAVONNE MUELLER's play, *Letters to a Daughter from Prison,* about Nehru and his daughter, Indira, was produced at the First

International Festival of the Arts in New York City and went on to tour in India. Her play *Violent Peace* was produced in London in 1992 and was the "Critics Choice" in *Time Out Magazine*. Her play *Little Victories* was produced in Tokyo by Theatre Classic Productions and directed by Riho Mitachi. Her play *The Only Woman General* was produced in New York City and went on to the Edinburgh Festival where it was "Pick of the Fringe" by the Edinburgh critics. She was awarded the Roger Stevens Playwriting Award, which she received at the Kennedy Center in Washington, D.C., in 1992. She is a Woodrow Wilson Scholar, a Lila Wallace Reader's Digest Writing Fellow, and has received a Guggenheim Grant, a Rockfeller Grant, three National Endowment for the Arts Grants, a Fulbright to Argentina, an Asian Culture Council Grant to Calcutta, India, and a U. S. Friendship Commission Grant to Japan. Her plays have been published by Dramatists Play Service, Samuel French, Applause, Performing Arts Journal, Theatre Communication Group, Heinemann, and Baker's Plays. Her textbook, *Creative Writing*, published by Doubleday and The National Textbook Company, is used by students around the world. She has taught at Columbia University for five years. As a Woodrow Wilson Visiting Scholar, she has helped colleges around the United States set up writing programs. She has been an Arts America speaker for the USIS (United States Information Service) in India, Finland, Romania, Japan, Yugoslavia, and Norway. She was recently a Fulbright Fellow to Jordan and received a National Endowment for the Humanities Grant to do research in Paris during the summer of 1995. Her play *American Dreamers* was selected for the book *Best Short Plays 1995–1996.*

CLIFFORD R. MURPHY is a very, *very* intelligent young man. He loves Elvis. He is a songwriter and rhythm guitarist for Say ZuZu, an insurgent country band from New Hampshire, who have recorded at Sun Studio in Memphis (where Mr. Murphy was fortunate enough to use the same rest room the King once used).

ANDRÉA J. ONSTAD has had her work read and workshopped at various theatres across the country: *Jukebox*, 450 Geary Theatre, San Francisco; *Colleen Clipped*, Padua Hills Playwright Workshop and Theatre of N.O.T.E. in Los Angeles and KBBK Studios and Eureka Theatre in San Francisco; *The House That Jack Built*, West Coast Playwrights, San Francisco, Theatre Artists of Marin, San Rafael, and the Vintage Theatre, New York; *Daddy's Daughters*, a short story choral performance, The Marsh, San Francisco; *Spirits on the Wind*, commissioned by People Speaking Theatre and read in various venues in the San Francisco area; *Leavin' on My Mind* and others, Victory Gardens, Chicago; *On the Subject of Eddie Gein, Necrophile, Murderer, Cannibal, or, Eddie, My Love*, The Playwrights Center, Minneapolis. She has held residencies at MacDowell, Yaddo, and most recently, the Vermont Studio Center for which she received a fellowship to the Fiction Writers Retreat. She has attended the Padua Hills Playwrights Workshop and Festival, and twice attended the Squaw Valley Community of Writers/Art of the Wind conference in fiction. She has received a Buck Grant in Playwriting and taught the Drama Workshop in the Master of Arts in Writing Program at the University of San Francisco and Beginning Playwriting to Emeritus Students at the College of Marin. She is a graduate of the University of Iowa Playwrights Workshop and a member of Throughline, a San Francisco playwrights group. She is currently working on several projects: *Over the Top*, a novella; *Tales from My Back Porch*, a collection of short stories; *Klep*, a full-length play; and *How He and She Got Married: A True Account as Written by Him and Her*, which she is also illustrating. She holds a full-time job as a legal secretary in a major San Francisco law firm and lives in Kentfield, California, with her husband, artist Peter Onstad, and their fourteen-year-old cat, Felicita.

LAURA QUINN decided to become a writer while still in kindergarten because it seemed like a neat thing to be. For a few years she got sidetracked and tried acting, but in the end decided that sending plays out was a lot less stressful than auditioning. She began writing plays at the University of Virginia, and received her MFA from the Playwrights Workshop at the University of Iowa. Her work has been presented by Playwrights Horizons, The Women's Project and Productions, New Georges, The Source Theatre Company of Washington, D.C., and Florida Studio Theatre, Sarasota. Her play, *Well Done Poets*, has been published by Broadway Play Publishing and was the winner of the Love Creek Productions Fifth Annual One-Act Festival. Her monologue "Fireweed" appears in *More Monologues for Women, by Women*, published by Heinemann.

LANIE ROBERTSON was awarded the 1987 Outer Critics Circle Award for his off-Broadway hit, *Lady Day at Emerson's Bar & Grill*. In 1993, he won the prestigious Kleban Award as Best Librettist for *Stringbean*, starring Leslie Uggams. Margot Kidder and Stacy Keach toured in Robertson's romantic comedy *Alfred Stieglitz Loves O'Keeffe* in 1995, and his thriller *A Penny for the Guy* had simultaneous productions last year at Virginia Stage Company in Norfolk and Studio Arena Theatre in Buffalo, NY. His published plays include *The Insanity of Mary Girard, Back County Crimes, Nasty Little Secrets*, and *Lady Day at Emerson's Bar & Grill*. His television work consists of the ABC Special for Diana Ross, *Red, Hot Rhythm 'n Blues*, and the American Playhouse film *Journey into Genius*, which starred Matthew Modine. *Nobody Lonesome for Me*, his new play, is scheduled for a Broadway production next season with Kevin Bacon.

SHARON HOUCK ROSS was awarded a 1996–1997 Disney Screenwriting Fellowship for the adaptation of her stage play *Trapped Daylight*. Her other plays include *Entry Points, A Melting Season, 11 Shades of White, Game!*, and *Summer Visits*, which have been produced by The Women's Project, New Georges, The Philadelphia Festival of New Plays, Colorado

Smokebrush Theatre, Circle Repertory Lab Theatre, the Iowa Festival of New Plays, and National Public Radio via the Iowa Radio Project. Sharon is a 1993 MFA graduate from the Iowa Playwrights Workshop at the University of Iowa.

MELISSA SCOTT is primarily a science fiction writer, which is excellent preparation for writing about Elvis. She hails from Little Rock, Arkansas, has degrees from Harvard College and Brandeis University, and has won science fiction's John W. Campbell Award for Best New Writer, as well as two Lambda Literary Awards for Gay/Lesbian Science Fiction, and has been short-listed for the James Tiptree Memorial Award. Elvis really did wink at her mother once, but none of the rest of it is true.

MICHAEL WRIGHT is head of playwriting and directing at the University of Texas at El Paso, and the director of the Play-Works festival, a new play development program. He is also the playwriting chair of Region VI of the Kennedy Center/American College Theatre Festival, and a resource artists for the WordBRIDGE Playwrights Laboratory in St. Petersburg, Florida. Recent publications include *The Student's Guide to Playwriting Opportunities* (Theatre Directories), *Playwriting in Process: Thinking and Working Theatrically* (Heinemann), *Payments and Debts* (Palmetto Play Service), *Sky Tumbling* (The Rio Grande Review), and *Bang! A Movie-Poem for the 90s* (Voces Fronterizas Anthology).

Performance Rights